The prince leans to the girl in scarlet heels,
Her green eyes slant, hair flaring in a fan
Of silver as the rondo slows; now reels
Begin on tilted violins . . .

Sylvia Plath, 'Cinderella', *Collected Poems*

For Keith and Joey

Acknowledgments

I am grateful to all the women who contributed their experiences in the preparation of this book. I would also like to express my appreciation for the support and encouragement of my friends and family.

Contents

THE GIRL IN SCARLET HEELS

Rachel Silver grew up in Jerusalem, studied Anthropology at University College, London and has written for television and the national press. Her first play, *Trapping the Antelope*, was staged at The Young Vic in 1986. She now writes for publications such as the *Telegraph Magazine*, the *Sunday Times* and *Woman's Journal*, and has recently made several documentaries for BBC Radio. Her previous books include *Establishment Wives*, published by W H Allen in 1989.

BY THE SAME AUTHOR

Establishment Wives
Wish Me Luck

THE GIRL IN SCARLET HEELS

Rachel Silver

C

Century · London

First published in Great Britain in 1993 by Century
Random House UK
20 Vauxhall Bridge Road, London SW1V 2SA

Century Hutchinson South Africa (Pty) Ltd
PO Box 337, Bergvlei 2012, South Africa

Random House Australia Pty Ltd
20 Alfred Street, Milsons Point, Sydney, NSW 2061
Australia

Random House New Zealand Ltd
18 Poland Road, Glenfield, Auckland 10
New Zealand

ISBN 0 7126 2179 2

Typeset by Pure Tech Corporation, Pondicherry, India

Printed and bound in U.K. by Clays Ltd., St Ives plc

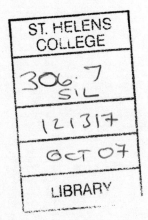

1

Twenty thousand orgasms

'I really love the idea that I produce twenty thousand erotic books and they're going to go out and produce twenty thousand orgasms,' said Tuppy Owens with relish. Tuppy became famous in the Sixties as a sex guru and now publishes the *Sex Maniac's Diary*. 'I couldn't believe that it was so easy to get money for jam,' remarked Helen Buckingham, describing her plunge into the murky waters of prostitution. 'I don't think anybody I've ever met felt they were damaged by it,' she continued. 'On the contrary, they felt that they were rescued by it.' These weren't quite the kind of views that I'd expected to hear when I began my research for this book. I had anticipated meeting people who were a bit secretive or unforthcoming, even ashamed or evasive.

'You mustn't think like that,' Tuppy Owens said emphatically when she rang me the day after our meeting, worried that perhaps I wasn't bold enough to put the case for the women in the sex industry to the world at large. Looking at prostitution, pornography, striptease and sex clubs in my role as writer, I found that people often had an antagonistic attitude towards me, and questioned my status because I was interested in women who worked in a business that was all about sex. When I met Tuppy I had put this to her. Did she feel that her involvement in the sex industry diminished her in the eyes of other people? She was, she said, beyond considerations of that nature. In fact I found, once I'd met and talked to other women in the business, that I was well off the mark. On the contrary, many of the women who work in pornographic films and as models in men's magazines, as editors of pornographic magazines, as nude dancers and strippers in clubs, call-girls and street-walkers, actually feel a powerful self-respect.

Perhaps I should make clear at the outset that this book started as an investigation into women who work as prostitutes. As I got further into my research I soon found that, for me, the issue was much broader than just prostitution. And after one particular meeting with a woman who acts in pornographic films, who I met by chance as she, an artist, was drawing the designs for a television programme I was working on, I realised that the real question was of women and their sexuality, and how they felt about making it work to their advantage, in any number of different ways.

I began to think that I could interview a series of women employed in selling sex, who were in control of their lives. It seemed to me that this was a logical result of feminism, that women should be in charge of their own sexuality and therefore able to exploit it. Why should men despise women who fulfil a need in society and at the same time are thereby enabled to live independent lives? I was born during the Sixties, and I feel that many of the battles of feminism have already been won, that women are freer today to be themselves than ever before – free to be independent career women, and to fulfil their desires.

Tuppy Owens, by any standards a sexually liberated woman, told me a story about an orgy she had attended in the Sixties. Like many women of her age remembering that era, she talked with a reminiscent smile. That evening, everyone was rushing off to have sex with each other. At one point a man forced himself on her and, although she protested, did not use a condom. Like men together at a rugby match, his friends laughed uproariously at her. 'Never mind,' they said, 'he's an abortionist.' She told me this story not, I think, to shock me. To her it was quite amusing and said something about men, though I think it did put her off attending this kind of gathering. It was simply something that had happened; but her suggestion that you had to take the rough with the smooth seemed to hang in the air.

This incident was described, during an interview, by a woman who seemed to have her sexuality well thought out. This was the sort of woman I had hoped would give a positive view of working within the sex business: a woman who was in control of her life and capable of making a good living in a world perceived to be one where men exploited women. And yet she had told me this story. I found it upsetting and I felt humiliated on her behalf. It seemed to me that liberation could, after all, sometimes backfire.

I had also thought that there was a clear line to be drawn between having sex for money and having the kind of sex that is about love and relationships. But, again, before I had got very far in my research, it was obvious that I would have to revise these assumptions. Morality in any kind of sexual activity is a piece of elastic; everyone has their particular way of dealing with their own limits. For example, using condoms for some prostitutes is a way of demarcating their relationships. The Praed Street Project at St Mary's Hospital in West London is a study of prostitute women who attend the clinic for the screening and treatment of sexually transmitted diseases. Ninety-six per cent of the women reported always using condoms for penetrative sex with clients. While a major fear was of infection, condoms also provided a means of keeping clients at a distance and making sex at work distinct from sex outside work. So the absence of a condom meant that for them, sex with their boyfriends was different, special. Eighty-two per cent reported not using condoms in their private lives. 'We have a very good sex life. It would be spoilt if he wore a sheath. We would be finished,' confirmed one prostitute. 'I don't want a stranger's come inside me.'

People are both fascinated and appalled by the notion of sex as a commodity. And sexual deviation is still anathema to Western society's view of the family. Prostitution and pornography are often condemned as an erosion of its values. The women who work in these covert professions are usually looked on with disapproval – and yet in many respects they continue to flourish. In a society which considers the emotional relationship to be its moral centre, the idea of paying for sex is officially repugnant and taboo. Cabinet ministers fall, Major Ronald Ferguson is disgraced, powerful men like the former Director of Public Prosecutions Allan Green resign in embarrassment. But nonetheless cars continue to kerb-crawl.

It has become more than a cliché to describe prostitution as 'the oldest profession'. Men have always liked looking at naked women, whether temple dancers in the centuries before Christ or, later, artists' models. Since biblical times, women, Mary Magdalen included, have been paid for sex. Often they worked in regulated brothels – in ancient Rome and Greece, even in medieval England. Interestingly, prostitution was outlawed in Britain only in the late nineteenth century, by which time it was so prevalent that an estimated one woman in every ten in London was on the game. To make a commercial enterprise out of their bodies and their sexuality has always been a fact of life for many women.

So who are the women involved, and why do they do it? What are their lives like? How can young women find it so unproblematic to contemplate modelling for Page 3 or setting out to excite crowds of men in strip clubs? Young or old, they are more often than not considered by many to be second-class citizens. What does this mean to them and how do they accept their own lifestyles? Is it different from, or can it be equated with – as many of the women I spoke to believe – the status of kept women or even some married women, whose husbands pay for their keep? Does love or the sanctity of a wedding ceremony make that much difference?

'I suppose,' admits David Hines, who in 1989 wrote the play *Bondage* about prostitution, 'that I too had the popular image of a prostitute in my mind. You know, that they enjoy it, or do it because they are bored, lonely, over-sexed and can earn money – all the excuses people make in order to create a caricature in place of a reality they don't want to face.' David Hines's play, which a year later was made into the film *Whore* by director Ken Russell, was a one-woman monologue about a night at King's Cross for a working prostitute, set out to expose the usual stereotypes and reveal the harsh reality. I felt that Hines had the right idea, discarding myth in favour of authentic grass-roots accounts. To some extent inspired by him, I set out to meet and talk to real people about their lives, and to let them tell their stories in their own words.

One of the strengths of Hines's play is to force the audience through a barrier of shock and convention, even embarrassment. Before an audience of strangers, the most intimate thing of all, our sexuality, is made public as the prostitute character talks specifically about sexual practices. She makes the audience squirm, by giving powerful insights into what the profession is actually about. And having cleared that barrier, the audience is able to appreciate, beyond the caricature image and sexual taboo, that these are indeed real women with real lives.

Geraldine, a nineteen-year-old working in Swindon, feels herself forced into prostitution for financial reasons. With three O-levels, she had a job with a furniture company but was quickly made redundant, and at the same time she found herself pregnant by a man who soon left. Now she has a baby son, Ashley. 'I hate to leave him, but I don't have a choice. You think I'd choose to do this?' she comments rhetorically. 'I'm giving men something they want for something I don't have: money. My kid has to eat. I've been arrested, lots of times, and I've been fined. More than £1000. The only way I can pay is to go on working. I've been beaten up and I've been raped. I think I can honestly say that I don't like blokes very much any more. I don't exactly see them at their best. How can you respect someone who produces a string of pork sausages and asks you to hit them over the backside with it?'

On the other hand Lisa, nineteen, working in Bradford, confesses that it was the 'easy money' that lured her into prostitution. 'My cousin's been on the game for ages. She always had lots to spend and I envied her. After losing my virginity I thought: What the hell? I might as well make money out of this. I've never found it difficult.' She lives with her boyfriend Steve, who she insists is not her pimp, and spends most of her money on new clothes. 'I'm not ashamed of what I do. I only do it for the money. The men don't matter to me. I'm totally detached from the sex. But I've done it for too long now to give up. I've never had any ambitions. It seemed inevitable I would end up on the dole.'

At the top end of the market there are women like Dolores French, wife of a barrister and author of *My Life as a Prostitute*, who glory in prostitution. She worked because she wanted to. And there are women like Sydney Biddle-Barrows, who ran a high-class escort service in New York for five years – until she was closed down by the police.

She felt that prostitution was akin to therapy. 'Like their counterparts in the other helping professions, our girls brought tenderness and comfort into our clients' lives. We were there for them. We listened to them. We made them feel better. We gave to them emotionally, and we gave to them physically. Sex may be its own reward, but touching and hugging are the most healing and life-enhancing activities in the world. Our society still needs to learn to tolerate the idea of women making a living by being intimate with men. Some people say that prostitution is degrading. Certainly it can be, but not in the agency I operated. I can think of a lot of jobs that are considerably more degrading than sharing an enjoyable evening with an attractive, successful man who is delighted to have you there and is willing to pay well for your company.'

How does prostitution affect women psychologically? Are they able to sustain normal relationships with other men, or are they incapable of doing so? How do they see men? Have their views of men altered since they've worked in the sex industry? What are their family backgrounds like? In chapter 7, I investigate the English Collective of Prostitutes, an organisation that campaigns for the abolition of the prostitution laws: 'By attacking the sexism which dooms most women to poverty and a twenty-four-hour working day, we lay the basis for prostitute and non-prostitute women to work together.' But can non-prostitute women comprehend and accept the lives of prostitutes?

An early experience in my research was an encounter on the telephone with the well known dominatrix Lindi St Clair. I arranged to meet the former 'Miss Whiplash' at two in the afternoon; working nights as she did, she explained, meant that she didn't get up till twelve noon, and certainly wasn't coherent till two. Any later than this, I said, and I'd have to bring my baby son with me. 'Oh no, dear,' she replied, 'you can't bring a child here, it's a brothel.'

On that basis I arrived alone, slightly late and flustered, as I couldn't find a parking space in Earl's Court. I eventually parked on her doorstep on a yellow line and rang the bell. She emerged in a pink track-suit; looking rather like a blancmange; she was short and tubby and her skin was puffy and white – clearly, here was someone who usually only ventures out at night. She stood pugnaciously on the doorstep. 'You're late. I allocated you half an hour. Your time's nearly up.' I felt a bit like one of her clients. 'You'd better tell me quickly what your questions are,' she went on. I stood beneath the big pink banner proclaiming 'The Corrective Party', and chatted briefly with her. I was obviously not going to get much detail about her life standing on the doorstep, so I arranged another appointment – for which she didn't turn up. Apparently she was too busy rehearsing the role of a client's wife in a play at the World's End pub in Chelsea. I subsequently discovered from Helen Buckingham, a former prostitute whom I did manage to interview, that Lindi did this sort of thing frequently. Helen knew her from appearing on television talk shows with her, and explained affectionately that Lindi always loved to act the street-wise, bossy tart. Apparently, keeping me loitering on the doorstep and then standing me up were just ways of exerting her need to dominate, a minor power game which mirrored the physical and financial control she held over the men who came to see her.

Having set out to deal with the whole range of commercial sexual activity, I turned from meeting prostitutes to looking at magazines, erotic books, videos, strip shows, massage parlours. And I met the women who were running these as efficient businesses.

I was soon initiated into the fascinating, sometimes bizarre and surprisingly emotional underworld of commercial sex in which women participate at all levels. 'Equality of the sexes doesn't mean you can't have sexuality,' comments the formidable Isabel Kaprowski, managing editor of the British *Penthouse*, *Forum* and the new women's pornographic magazine *For Women*. 'Women are queuing up to appear in *Penthouse*. We put them on a pedestal, make them look as beautiful as possible. There's nothing wrong with that: women can be intelligent as well as sexy. We are very exhibitionistic: we learn early on that it's one of our areas of power. We like to turn a few heads when we go into a room and I think it's just an extension of that. Sex permeates pop music, film, TV, yet society separates off porn and applies different criteria to it.'

But Nina Lopez-Jones, spokeswoman for the English Collective of Prostitutes, has a more sombre view regarding prostitution. 'Actually, in most cases it's simply a means of making ends meet. Because ours is a sexual activity, people forget we're on the game for the money. At least seventy per cent are mothers. They see prostitution as a way not to descend into poverty. Men do all kinds of things for money; more ways are open to them than to women.'

Approaching the project, I did feel a certain apprehension because I didn't know what I was going to find. Perhaps I would be probing into people's lives in a way they might very much resent; would I meet with physical violence? But in fact what I did do was meet individuals who were all complex and sophisticated characters with their own points of view. My initial worries were turned on their heads, and I came to believe that there is no reason why women should not have every right to call the shots in the commercial sexual domain in the way they now do in their private lives.

2

Mostly they make me laugh

'What I'm doing now isn't prostitution – it's therapy. And I never fuck, they don't touch my body, none of my clients touch my body. I work on them, because some people don't understand that this is pleasurable, even touching the neck and the shoulders and the tips of the fingers, and I try to get them in touch with the feelings in the nerves and the blood and the muscles in their body, and to visualise themselves being well and healthy, whole people, and to feel right about sex. And to go out and make relationships that stay.'

In her late thirties, Bella is small, dark and vivacious; originally from Iran, she's lived in England since she was eighteen. We talked as we sat in the comfort of her East London brothel, in a flat reached via a metal fire-escape, off a run-down parade of shops. The lounge was lavishly furnished with thick pink carpets and matching sofas, boxes of chocolates open on the glass coffee table. Framed black and white photographs of women adorned the walls. The effect was striking and artistic – the sort of pleasant image you can find in any high-street poster shop. But I noticed that tucked into the mirrors and on the mantelpiece were snaps of Bella and her partner in kinky sexual attire; large breasts and thighs spilling out from under and over tight black leather garments presented a strained, provocative show of strength. Bella's thick-set friend Maureen, who shared the same premises, had come in soon after I arrived and had sat down with us still in her heavy wool coat, which remained buttoned to the neck. I looked at the two women sitting there in their everyday clothes, and found it hard to reconcile the photos with the reality. Maureen was miserable with a cold and blew her nose a lot. Turning to glare at me occasionally, she was clearly not pleased about my visit.

9

'I feel so fulfilled,' Bella continued, looking poised and elegant in her black blouse and skirt and with her face carefully made up – she said she always made up her face for work – 'making so many people happy and earning a living. It is now no longer my profession, it is now my vocation, and I'm very fortunate to have discovered that my mission in life is to be doing what I am. I mean, I'm a tart. My husbands have always liked tarts as their wives – all my exes – or they wouldn't have been with me. I'm very honest, I don't put on airs, graces. I know a lot of women that do.' I asked what her present husband feels about her work. 'Yesterday he couldn't have enough of me, last evening was wonderful. He thinks it's wonderful, isn't it marvellous how good I'm looking? because I'm obviously feeling good.'

As she said this everything seemed to make sense in the quiet sitting room. But wasn't it all illegal? 'It is, it is stupidly illegal, believe it or not. My friend here does one sort of therapy, I do another sort. She gets people in touch with the darker side of life, but if anyone were to walk in here, the reporters or the police, they would call it a brothel, because we two happen to be working here and it has a little bit to do with sex. It's not sexually orientated completely. I mean, if anyone wants a straight fuck they've come to the wrong place, because they're not going to get it here, they're not going to get straight sex here. They are going to be able to explore their inside as well as their bodies. And yet this would be considered a brothel. That's the stupid laws we have. Our address here has to be hidden. I couldn't put ads in and say, "Come to our clinic and explore the light and the dark of your life." I'd love to do that, but I couldn't.'

She was happy to explain how she had stumbled into the sex business. 'At the age of seventeen or eighteen I got into nude modelling. I was involved with a foreign man and needed the money to go to see him. My father was a pilot and I grew up in India. Then he was posted to Seattle to do jungle training, so I was in America for a year and then came back here, and decided I would go to France as an au pair. I then went to Bombay for a holiday and met a Yugoslav sailor and fell in love and decided I would scrap Paris altogether. Later my parents were posted to England for five years, so I joined

10

them. This only lasted three months but I did lots of nude modelling in that time because I had these huge tits. These are them' – she gestures down unnecessarily. 'I had them made smaller but they've grown back again, almost to the same size they were before. I breast-fed my son for two years after I had the operation and they went very small after I stopped breast-feeding. And then after a year they grew back again!

'At nineteen I went to live in Yugoslavia with the sailor, but he was very, very violent – though he's a very good friend of mine now. No one spoke English. I learned Serbo-Croatian, but then I'd had enough and four months later I came back to live with my parents and that's when I decided I would try being a whore.'

'Viva la sex industry,' Bella proclaimed with enthusiasm, as she put a kettle on to boil in the small kitchen and searched for mugs and tea-bags. She then explained how she had come to make that decision. 'I saw the ads in the *Evening Standard*. They wanted hostesses – I didn't know what a hostess was and I rang and asked, and they said, "Well, you sit there and chat with a man, you drink champagne, and you get paid." You get paid something like ten or fifteen pounds in 1974, just to sit and talk and dance and drink champagne, and I thought that can't be bad . . .

'My first night was disastrous,' she admitted as we sat down to drink our tea. 'The women were hard and ugly and cold and horrible. Most of the prostitutes there – at the club on Bruton Street, London – they asked me if I was "going case", and I hadn't a clue what "going case" meant. And "going case" of course means sleeping with the clients. They said I was too innocent and it was ridiculous, and I was nineteen and a half, nearly twenty by then. I was interested in the work, I wasn't quite happy about it, but I needed the money. I was having problems with a boyfriend and I didn't want to ask my parents for money. They could have given it to me, but I chose not to ask them. Eventually in my tears I met a man who paid me twenty quid to leave, so I did. I left the club rapidly with him, the twenty pounds in my pocket, and thought I'd done very well – that was how I started.

11

'The girls were then asking thirty pounds for a fuck and I said I wouldn't go for under seventy-five. I did get a few clients for seventy-five, though everyone else was thirty. When they asked me what was different I said I wasn't so hard, I had youth, I was a human being. I wasn't a hard, cold machine like that. And I got my money. In fact I had a very nice Swedish lover from that time; I always make lovers out of clients. I was a lousy whore in so far as I couldn't ask for the money. I was never embarrassed to take off my knickers and fuck with them. But I was always embarrassed to ask them for money, very stupid.'

One of the girls I was put in touch with, Jay, in her late twenties, was reluctant to speak to me, saying that she didn't like the idea of journalists making money out of her life. Eventually she agreed to meet me at a café near Leicester Square in London. She apparently had had a similar background to many of the people I had been to university with, but she hadn't enjoyed herself. A girl from a small Norfolk village hungry for excitement but soon disillusioned by the inevitable student poverty and the rigours of exams at Goldsmith's College, London. After the misery of an abortion she had dropped out and moved in with a crowd of young people, most of whom were now in prison. 'I never liked university, I was only there because my parents pushed me. Once I was free of my mother I suddenly realised I didn't have to stay there.' She didn't explain how, or really, why she'd decided to be a prostitute. Perhaps she had never really made a decision – just floated into it, needing money.

'My first experience was terrible. The man was very rough, he knew I hadn't done it before. He took advantage of me, did stuff that you'd never do with a client, only with a lover. I've worked in lots of different places, but for me it's better on the street. You pretend less on the street, there's none of this fake affection – you just do it. I can't stand the idea of men thinking we're both getting pleasure out of it. For me it's a job like any other job. I could move on – I could if I didn't need the money, the bills to pay every month.'

She wanted to know whether I'd had boyfriends who'd bought me dinner or given me presents expecting sex in return, and wasn't it the same thing? She seemed angry that she was where she was in her life. 'The law is shit, it's a joke. They should leave us alone. The police make it more dangerous for us.' I asked her what she hoped for her future. 'I often think about living in a house and having a husband and children. I feel like I'm a split personality, the girl who came from the country and wants to go back there, but then mostly people don't want to know me now.'

I paid for the coffee after she'd gone. And I sat for a little longer in the café wondering how much of her anger was aimed at herself and how much of it was caused by the job she did. It had been a tense meeting and my overall impression was that she probably would rather not have met me. She had left abruptly, not at all willing to talk about the physical details of her job or to put me in contact with anyone else.

Bella, on the other hand, was forthcoming. I wondered about the times when things had got threatening or out of hand. 'I was locked in a room overnight by some horrible Pakistani guy who kept threatening me. He was drunk. Fortunately, there was another girl with me. We had come from a night-club, and when I reported him to the manager of the night-club they didn't do anything about it as he was a regular there. So influence and money buy more than poor whores. Also, once in the Dorchester a man attacked me with an oyster knife, and I punched him in the balls with my knee and ran off. Probably there've only been three threatening events in years, but then I only ever did the street three days of my life. I tried the street outside a large London hotel.'

This experience she found exciting. 'It was wonderful, I was young and dressed like a real tart. I thought: I have to look like a tart when I'm going on the street. I did myself up as a tart, wore a bright-red jacket with a little mini-skirt, and over-made-up – very nicely made up but over-made-up – and got off the bus at the hotel. Within two minutes I got my first man following me down the street. He said, "Don't look behind you, there's a policeman there. I'm in the hotel, room 307 – just follow me up." So I did.

'I came out of his room half an hour later and in the lift I met a second client, and I came out of the second client's room half an hour later and met the third, so it was a very good evening. Three people, and by ten-thirty I was back in the hotel lift. I charged about thirty-five pounds a screw, but this is going back years.

'But I only did it for three days because I thought that it was dangerous, and I heard all sorts of stories. Also, on the third day I was approached by security at the hotel. They'd kept an eye on me, and they said, "Was I working their area?" And I didn't know anything about this – I was quite innocent. So I just ran and never came back. And then I joined a night-club. In fact, after doing the rounds of night-clubs I found one in which I was very happy, as happy as one could be in a night-club. I was never really happy. It's like the cattle trade. You sit in a row, you really learn lessons in humiliation. You have people look you up and down and not choose you one night, and everyone else is booked out and you're not, and you have to learn that this is part of the game – nothing to be ashamed of that you don't happen to be chosen one night. You wouldn't get paid if you weren't chosen. But when you did get paid you only got paid a minimum payment for the hostess work. The money you made was going back with them afterwards to fuck them.

'I worked there for seven months and then I joined an escort agency and that was nice. I knew the man who ran the escort agency and his girlfriend and it was a much more homely affair. The escort was an evening out. You always had dinner. You got about a hundred pounds, for a dinner and drink and a fuck. And conversation and everything. It was safe and you met a nicer class of client, and you made regulars there as well.'

When I met Lorraine, who is a secretary in her twenties, she had been working part-time for an escort agency for the past seven months. Of mixed race, she is remarkably beautiful, tall and slim with a shock of curly black hair. She speaks with a London accent and comes across as bright but not particularly articulate. We sat at a small table in a pub off the Fulham Road in South West London, she was friendly though apparently slightly embarrassed that an acquaintance of mine had pointed her out at a drinks party as being the beautiful 'escort' that a rich but physically unappealing contact of his had brought along. On her way to an escort job at a discreet Chelsea hotel, she was smartly dressed. 'The money isn't very good as a secretary. I'm hoping to save now and be able to go and work in New York – I've been there before. I did some promotional demonstrations there and I'm saving to go back. I do escort work a couple of nights a week. It's not something I talk about very much.'

I asked her if the escort work was like going out on a date – a male friend of mine had described his evening with a girl from an escort agency in this way. 'Put it like this: for me it's work, you know what you're there for. Mostly they make me laugh. I never decided to make money this way. I don't call myself any names. I wouldn't give up being a secretary. I'm happy with what I do – I'm not doing it for much longer.'

She was in a hurry, and becoming nervous about talking to me. I attempted to walk her up the road, but she rapidly hailed a cab and disapeared off down the Fulham Road.

Bella soon moved on from the escort service to do more lucrative work. 'I joined with a madam that I met in a night-club – a very nice lady, who asked how much I got and I said a hundred pounds for the evening. And she roared with laughter and said, "Come to me and get two fifty." And I did too. I worked with her for four months until I was tired of being buggered and screwed by Arabs. Those were the days when the Arabs were flourishing, the Seventies. I got tired of working with Arabs. I was also doing nude modelling and porno films all along, on the side, as well as doing whoring.'

Was she happy, looking back at that stage of her life? 'Absolutely, yes, exactly. And no one was coercing me into anything. I think the only thing that's immoral, highly immoral, is to have someone coerced into anything. I'm totally anti snuff movies, child pornography, even some animal films which I've seen where the animals obviously don't look like they want to do it. I'm very anti anything that is coercing, but as far as I'm concerned if people want to do whatever they're doing, it's their life and they should be allowed to do it.'

15

What about her family? Did her parents know what she was doing? 'Oh no, my parents hadn't a clue, they would have died. My mother saw a nude picture of me in *Penthouse* and died. She never talked to me for four months.' But she read *Penthouse*? I queried. 'My father read *Penthouse*, and yet he had double standards. I pointed out to them the double standards, and it took them four months to get over it, and then talk to me again. But, I mean, they'd given me large sums of money. They bought me a house. It wasn't like they weren't supporting me financially. And my father was a little shocked when my ex, the violent Yugoslav boyfriend, told him I was a whore. He mentioned it six months later: "Milan said you are a whore. What's the going rate?" And when I told him he wasn't so embarrassed about me being a whore after all.' She laughed at the memory.

'People have double standards all the time,' she continued. 'And I believe now, in my thirty-eighth year of life, that my mission is to break down these barriers, this hypocrisy, these double standards.'

The years of prostitution didn't seem to have hardened her. I had seen for myself that the older women parading sullenly on my local West London streets looked dreadfully tired and worn. 'The hard women are usually the women who work in clubs, and I don't see many hard women in the escort agencies – a few in the escort agencies but never when they're doing private jobs. It's rare to have met hard women who do private jobs. I don't know why. I think it's really to do with the personality one has anyway.

'They're hardened because they're not integrated into their sexuality. I enjoy sex. I enjoyed it with nearly every client, a lot of clients. Those that wanted me to give them pleasure, I enjoy giving pleasure, I enjoy taking pleasure. I really appreciate my clients, I respect them. Gone are the days when I will go with anyone. Now I don't fuck with anyone anyway – Aids and all that, there's no point. But there came a time when I decided to respect the clients who I go with and I've had a few regulars for the last fifteen or sixteen years. I have three people that I've seen for sixteen years now. It's been a good life. It's been all right. I've been confused and muddled, but

16

Buddhism has saved me from all that. It's given me deep insight into myself and into the mechanics of everyday mundane life – whether someone is a sweeper or a rich tycoon or a prostitute I can see a way in, I can get an intimate insight into the mechanics of life and how life works and make it work for me with supreme happiness, and spread supreme happiness around as well. It's very nice because I've integrated the mind and the body and the spirit.'

Bella's view of prostitutes as therapists spreading happiness seemed to me to be a controversial one. After all, traditionally the prostitute is not seen as a therapist but as a fallen woman, with a status lower than that of other women in society. 'You're right, it is lower. It's something that society has to come to terms with. It is after all the oldest profession, it *is* a profession. A good prostitute is not only a prostitute. She is a very good actress and she's a counsellor, she's a therapist, she's to do with the pleasures – or pain, depending on the angle she's taking in the business. I think it's very sad that society has to put them down. I think that if the woman sees herself as lower then indeed she is lower. If a woman sees herself as being good for what she's doing, then she is indeed. I command much more respect now because I don't have low self-esteem any more, which I did have for many years – just mirroring society's views.'

Bella is completely open about the work she does, making a point of telling everyone. 'People can try and put me down. If they put me down in a reasonable way and wish to discuss how they feel, then I'm very open to discussion and I'm very respectful of their opinion of me, be it low. But if people just want to give me criticism for the sake of criticism without having thought it out, then they are just putting up Aunt Sallys which I could knock down with a breath, just one breath.'

She went on to tell me about the next stage of her life, after she had tired of the Arabs 'and of behaving like an idiot having a birthday for them. If you had the tiniest bit of intelligence working with an Arab they wouldn't want you. You had to behave like an idiot with no brains and a body. They expected you to behave in a silly way and giggle and say things like "One for the road", in a silly, cutesy, adoring way, or "Just a little kiss", like you would if it were a birthday. And unfortunately I was never very popular with them because I couldn't behave so well like an idiot. So I went back to the Madam and I said, "I'm giving up whoring." And she said, "Oh, once a whore always a whore." And maybe she was right, but I decided I would give up. One of my colleagues, an American lady from Oregon, wanted me to be her mistress – in private life we were having an affair – and she was very submissive and I was the dominant partner. I'd never learnt about this but she taught me a little bit, and she suggested to me that we do live shows for the Arabs, with the Madam. So the Madam said, "Very interesting – give us a sample of your show." So Kay and I put on this show and Madam got turned on, and Madam was not usually turned on. She said, "Great, I'll sell this. Two hundred and fifty okay for you?" Great for me, forty-five minutes' work, no man touching you. Great, no problem.

'Unfortunately the shows were always after the casinos, and it was about three or four o'clock in the morning in the Dorchester or wherever. And we would do the shows with all the other girls the Madam would bring in tow, and the punters would get excited and screw the girls, and I would get my rate and that was it. My girlfriend got her rate for screwing the men as well as for the show, because she could make lots of money that way. She's very wealthy now, she's bought a house. She spent her money very sensibly – unlike me, easy come easy go, I gave away most of it. I have nothing to show for those years, nothing, nothing.'

In a way this was deliberate, though perhaps at the time only subconsciously so. 'I blew it on stupidity, on friends, entertainment, parties, entertaining people all the time. I didn't even spend it on myself. Crazy – I blew it on other people. Because the whole thing made me bloody miserable, I didn't understand myself. A waste of time, a total waste of time for me to have done that – I didn't have anything to show for it, I wasn't developing as a character. I was underdeveloping, I was stagnating, I was going into regression instead of progress.'

Working as a prostitute did to some extent have a negative effect on Bella's private life. There had been men in her life who had tried to use her and live off her high, cash income. 'All the men in my life always knew what I was doing right from day one. I lived with a man, a journalist, a writer, for some time, and he was paying his estranged wife all the money he earned for a year while I was keeping him, until I said I was tired of keeping him and I didn't want another ponce – this was the second time it had happened – so he gave up his job and became a student. And I then left prostitution completely for six years. I was twenty-three and I joined the art business. I bought and sold Japanese woodblock prints and I got trained by a lovely man that I met socially. He needed someone to help him out because he doesn't live in this country, and I did the European, the Western, side of the world – it was just buying and selling, mostly at auctions and private collections.

'After six and a half years I left my art job because the guy expected me to do hours and hours a day of cataloguing as well as going to the auctions, and I wanted more salary. He wouldn't give me more salary and I thought well, bugger it, my husband could afford to keep me, I wouldn't work – though all this time I had been doing some sexual therapy work with disabled people on a voluntary basis, which I kept up. I met my husband when I was twenty-two, while I was a lady of the night. I told him at our first meeting, and he spat out his gin and tonic and said, "My God, are you always that honest?" And I said yes – I mean, I don't make friends, I make clients. I thought he would be a client, but he fell in love with me and I fell in love with him. He's now my ex-husband and we're still friends.

'After I left the art business a friend got me a job which lasted for four months. I was to be companion to this lady who had a very, very rich lover or husband or whatever. He was one of the richest men in the world and all I had to do was to accompany her to fashion shows and things, very boring. I was with her twice a week and getting this huge salary – it was his way of giving to the charity for disabled people as he knew I worked doing a kind of sex therapy with these people, when I wasn't working for him. And I made an awful mistake – I told him he should find me some more work

19

because I couldn't justify the money I was earning, and he paid me a month in advance and said, "Leave." A shame, I lost my little income there for my stupidity.

'Then I didn't do much work. I did a little bit of counselling, a sort of sex surrogate work which I got from the late Dr Morris Jaffe at Guy's Hospital. He died two years ago. Sex surrogacy is helping people with problems. For example, I had a man who really wanted to be married, a rich Jewish boy, only son of a rich family who expected to get married and have children. He couldn't get it up with a woman because his fantasies all surrounded boys' hands. I had to retrain him into allowing himself to fantasise but at the same time being with a woman, and I would hold his penis and tell him to use his fantasies so that he wouldn't have to tell his wife the fantasies but be able to use them to please her and to have a happy marriage and get his way at the end. And he's very happy. I have a few people who are very happy now that I worked with, from various doctors, who'd send me people.'

Bella's ideas of therapy and well-being and finding herself through God and her adopted religion, Buddhism, combine into a philosophy of integration of mind, body and spirit.

'I like to share my philosophy with my clients now. Very nice to see them going away happy – I want them to, I want them to know that they've been fulfilled in their lives. Now I already have some regulars. I've only been going here for three weeks and I've had three coming back again. And they will, they'll be regular until they're strong enough to stand on their own two feet and they don't need to ever pay for it again. That's my aim, except for massage – I do a relaxing massage. These are people who have never been able to make and maintain a long-term permanent relationship, which is a very fulfilling thing to have in life, and I try and show them how to do this, over sessions, slowly. I work with them on this because I was trained by Chad Vara, who founded the Samaritans, in counselling. And I hope they'll always come back for the massage. Three people have said in the last two days that they've felt really wonderful after the massage, they've been walking on air. I put a lot of energy into the massage, and I refuse to allow any talking during it.

'When I left my first husband because it just wasn't working out, I got a regular secretarial office job which was very dull and it lasted two and a half years. It was soul-destroying. And then I stopped work to have my son James with my new husband. And I didn't work at all for a few years. Then I got a little part-time job selling paints and things for houses in Texas Homecare stores, and other boring, badly paid jobs like that. And so my husband said, "Oh, you look so depressed. This is all soul-destroying – why don't you do what you do best?" And I said, "You know what I do best. I relate to people best, and it's best for me to be working for myself." And he wasn't sure then, so I didn't do anything about it. Then last year I met some photographers, a couple of them, who said I was looking great and would I like to do some more nude modelling? So I did some nude modelling last year. I met a few kind people like the friend I rent this flat with, who gave me the odd job in the sex trade, but not fucking– wanking and meeting men and what have you. And then she said she had an extra room, why didn't I work here? So I started putting ads in and got replies and . . .'

Bella took me out of the sitting-room and briefly along a corridor to see her work-room which, she explained, she was only just setting up. At first glance it looked like a cross between a Nautilus gym and a torture chamber, though perhaps my initial negative impression had more to do with the fact that I hate that whole gym-cum-beauty-therapy-centre ethos, and one look at a long bench covered in black plastic (or perhaps it was leather) was enough to remind me unpleasantly of attempts to get fit via pumping weights, or of that dreadful helpless feeling you get when having your face steamed. But Bella was clearly proud of her professional apparatus, and I imagined that with the light dimmed, lying on that bed and abandoning oneself to the tender mercies of Bella's soothing finger-tips, with no distracting clutter about, would indeed be a relaxing and unfrightening experience.

I had no idea how you'd go about advertising this sort of service. Did she put ads in the men's magazines? 'No I don't, I put ads in the *Sunday Sport*. David Sullivan, the owner, gave me the idea of what to do and it worked – the lonely hearts column of the *Sport*, and it only costs me two pounds. The ads say little things like this: 'Comely and curvy ex-model, trained counsellor and masseuse, invites women, men and TVs [Transvestites] to enjoy a pleasure therapy of body, mind and spirit.' Or, 'Exotic-looking ex-model, trained counsellor, masseuse and sex therapist, offers a comprehensive all-person service to women and men looking to end their lonely-heart problems.' She showed me the relevant page in that week's paper, pleased to note that her advertisement was in.

'I got loads of replies, from one ad. I got thirty-five replies, of which ten were genuine. Some people mistook the ad and thought I would be a girlfriend to end their lonely-heart problems, so they didn't take it as a therapy, but those that did were good.' How much does this therapy cost? 'It depends – it depends on how long people take. It could be anything from twenty-five pounds, which was all I charged one poor student, to my usual rate of a hundred pounds. I don't want to reject people just because they don't have the money. This is after all my vocation as well as my profession. The money is important but it's not all-important.'

Through much of her life, Bella admits, she has had difficulties in integrating her sexuality with the other elements of herself. 'Through all those years I was still searching for myself. I went to retreats, Christian retreats. I met some wonderful Christian people, and then I got pregnant in between that. I had a little stillborn baby boy – he was stillborn at seven months. So I was lying in hospital, aged twenty-three, feeling dreadful, feeling very sorry for myself. And I saw a rabbi pass, and I called the nurse and I said, "Could I see a minister of any religion? Doesn't matter which", but she said, "But what religion are you?", and she insisted, so I said Zoroastrian, the religion I was born into. She thought I'd said Austrian, so she got me a Catholic priest. I saw him, a lovely man, and I said, "Please don't give me mumbo-jumbo, just a talk to me as one intelligent person to another." And he was delightful. He sat with me and explained that for every part that dies another is resurrected. He was lovely, and three days later I experienced what I still today, as a Buddhist now, feel. I experienced the Christ within. I experienced this feeling

22

of absolute love, this ocean of love, and I was swimming in it, being rocked by it on waves of love. There was no room for pain, there was no room for sorrow.

'That was it, it wiped out all the sorrow in one go. The reward was much greater than the loss, and I was very grateful to be given this wonderful thing. The price I paid was minimal – this wonderful experience that few have, that realising, knowing at one moment your own Christ nature, what I call my Buddha nature now. It was wonderful. The professor in charge of me at the time, because I had so many gynaecological complications, was just amazed. He said, "Your philosophy is so strong. Some women suffer years of depression – look at you, four days later and you're laughing." So it's great, I am a blessed child, I'm a fortunate child, I'm very blessed, I have a charmed life.'

I tried hard to understand what Bella was saying to me, but having had a stillborn baby myself I found her view hard to comprehend. I was devastated and numbed when my son was born dead, and the experience traumatised me for a long time. In fact, it was not until my second son was born four years later that I was able to move on in my life and live with it. I probed further, as we discussed her feelings, and found that other feelings had indeed been there alongside.

'I had thought at first the baby had been taken from me as a punishment for all the very many abortions I'd had,' she said slowly. 'Then I stopped thinking of it like that. I thought it was an angel come down to give me a message – it was very good, it was an angel of hope, my stillborn boy. And I really willed him out of me. I was so insecure and my husband at the time didn't want children and I knew it would all be on me, and I was most unfair to the child. I offer an apology to this little child every day now for the way I felt about it, it was positively ugly – my attitude to that child was ugly. I had wanted to be pregnant but I was so insecure, I knew I'd get no help from the man, and the whole thing scared the life out of me. Now, with my second child, if I was all on my own I know that I could cope, that I would love this child, come what may. But with that one I wasn't sure. And I was miser-able and I willed it out of me, and then when I lost it it was a shock. I couldn't make up my mind . . .'

23

This made me wonder about those other, positive, feelings she had shown earlier, which might be veiling grief and loss, or which might be an expression of the difficult status of women who work in the sex business. And yet I wouldn't doubt her generosity and kindness, her genuine concern for people with sexual problems.

When I began to research this book I didn't really know what to expect from the women I met. When Bella invited me to her home for a buffet dinner with her family and friends over the Christmas break, it was clearly a gesture of friendship. It was a private family get-together in Bella's and her husband's pleasant South London home, with wonderful cooking and Christmas festivities. But her professional side was still apparent; there was an openness amongst the guests in their ability to discuss sexuality, and I came away at the end of the evening with some surprising Christmas gifts, such as a vibrator – something I'd not been given before – and a little book of sexy cartoons from a charming and intelligent blind man. The philosophy that Bella has achieved may well be a response to the world that she has lived in since she was a young girl. She has certainly succeeded in finding her own place in the sex world, one that allows her to be a generous and open-hearted person.

'When are they going to legalise all this?' was her instant and passionate response when I asked if there was anything she particularly felt ought to be said on the subject of prostitution. 'I am very fulfilled, and if Mary Whitehouse or anybody else would like to say I'm not, then I challenge them to come and hold a reasonable debate with me where it's not a slanging match, where I'm not throwing shit around them and they're not slinging nastiness towards me, but where we can sit as reasonable civil human beings and hold a dialogue.

'I trained with Chad Vara for two and a half years – he knows what I do and how I use the wonderful training I've had from him. He's eighty years old now, and he's a wonderful man. He's devoted his life to helping others and he was the first sex therapist in this country, and one of the pioneers of the permissive society. I'd be very happy to hold a dialogue with any of the anti-sex people.'

3

No Angel

'In what ways am I not an angel?' Karen gesticulated widely, a vivid spectacle in thigh-high boots and figure-hugging jeans. Sitting on the red-plush bench of our local pub, in Maida Vale she was excited and chatty. Her mobile and attractive face, framed by her long, straight, dark hair, was animated as she considered. 'I don't know where to start! I like erotica too much to be an angel, and I've had too many boyfriends to be an angel. I'm an exhibitionist. I'll take my clothes off in a straight club if somebody dares me, I'm not shy or anything. My worst thing is, if someone says I bet you wouldn't do such and such, I'll do it. Bob's much more reserved than I am. It would be quite a normal thing for me to get under a table in a restaurant to him, but he gets put off.

'When I first met Bob, my boyfriend, he knew I did strip-tease but he'd never been to see me at work, and he asked me to do him a striptease when we'd just got together as boyfriend and girlfriend. I was terribly embarrassed. I can get up and do a striptease in front of two thousand men, but could I do one for him on his own in our living-room? I couldn't do it. It was really embarrassing – I was like a little girl, all silly and stupid and giggly and I just couldn't do it. And that's the difference, that's the real me doing striptease. Funnily enough, another night he asked me to do it and I'd had a bit to drink as well and I found I could do it that night because we'd been out and I'd been wearing a wig and I looked very different. And I still felt different and I managed to do it, with a little bit of drink and looking different, but he got a different version, a different performance! But when he eventually came to see me at work he liked my act. He'd been to see hundreds of stripteases anyway – he's well into going to that sort of thing, and into the magazines, though

25

I think with my work I've now taken a lot of the fun out of it for him.'

During the evening I briefly met Bob, a good-looking black man in his early thirties who makes his living running a fetish club. He ambled in to join us in the pub, wondering good-naturedly what Karen was going to do about supper. She immediately gave him firm instructions about which vegetables to get from the corner shop and how to cook them. I liked Karen. We sat there together, approximately the same age, thirtyish, and living in the same part of West London. She had an unmistakable energy and enthusiasm for life. I had been introduced to her originally as someone I would find interesting because she had been trying to organise a union for strippers. Her concern for ensuring a fair wage for doing a strip was the key to understanding her view of her profession. I wondered how stripping in clubs had changed her view of men.

'I do tend to pigeon-hole men when I first meet them – I don't mean a boyfriend, it could just be a man I've met with a group of friends or whatever – I tend to pigeon-hole them. I can see what sort of a punter they'd be if they were in my shows. Are they a first row? A second row? Are they a pain in the arse? Are they a groper? Are they difficult? Are they a mouthy one that shouts abuse? I don't know whether I do it consciously or not but I can just see them somewhere in an audience, what they would be like when their wives or girl-friends aren't there. They're different animals when they don't have their women around them, especially *en masse* – you see them at their ugliest, you really do.'

There was no seediness about this modern young woman. I asked why she had continued stripping over the years. 'I've carried on doing the job because not all jobs are ugly and threatening, and it's very hard to stop, it's like a drug. Not this year, because this year's been abysmal, but up until now, when you are doing it the money is usually good, or it *was* good up until a couple of years ago. So by then for someone like myself – I already had commitments like with a house and all the rest of it – I couldn't suddenly stop doing it and get a job that would earn me the same amount of money, having never trained for anything.

'I started when I was eighteen, I had O-levels and A-levels, but I was never trained for anything, so to suddenly turn up at twenty-eight and say that I want a job that's going to earn me the same money that I earn doing striptease, without any higher qualifications or work experience, is very difficult. So you really do get stuck, you're in like a catch-22. I think it's the same for a lot of girls in the sex industry and women who are prostitutes as well. It becomes like a drug and they can't see a way out of it.'

It is hard to imagine the benefits outweighing the drawbacks in this kind of work. Karen's job is to arouse large groups of men, a situation in which the danger of rape is genuine. What is it, I asked, that she actually does on stage? 'Legally you've got to keep one foot on the stage at all times, and you're not allowed to have contact with the audience. However, nobody sort of takes that to the full. People do walk round the audience – they expect it, they'd go mad if you didn't. And I do involve the audience, asking them to undo a suspender or something, all sorts of silly things. In my Pink Panther spot I get a chap up, I blindfold him and then I produce an inflatable doll, an elephant, and I put his hand on the elephant's trunk and make him give it a wank in time to the music – he can't see what he's doing, but of course everyone else can see. I even open his mouth and stick the elephant's trunk in it – just really silly things – or I get a banana while he's sat there and make him hold it in front of him, here [she gestured], and then I go down and I give the banana a blow job, and at the end I tell him to open his mouth so that I can feed him, and I shove it all in his mouth so that he chokes. I'm quite lethal, I am! I enjoy it if the audience are happy and good. If the audience are really drunk and miserable then I don't enjoy it.'

A few days later I went to one of the smaller clubs that Karen performs at, a basement hostess club in the centre of London, just off Charing Cross Road. It was dark, with a cluster of tables in the middle of the room and booths around the walls. There were not very many customers about and those that were there were mostly huddled in booths, talking to girls. When a black girl dressed as a leopard entered with her only prop, a chair, I expected her act would be as tacky as the surroundings. However, I admired her grace and dancing ability, her lithe dancer's body that any woman would envy. When she began to do her strip a few heads looked up; she moved slowly and I did find it quite erotic. She finished her five-minute spot, totally nude and draped dramatically over the chair – in a way, quite stunning. When I tried to find her to interview her I discovered that she had already sped off to her next five-minute gig at another club. She would regularly work at three different clubs in an evening, making a good living out of it.

On a subsequent evening I had a drink after her show with a dancer who did a non-strip dance number at the Charing Cross Road club. Sue has been a professional dancer on the club circuit for a couple of years, trying to make it as an artist. But she said wryly, 'Often the punters yawn during our acts waiting for the strippers. We always think of ourselves as artistic.' Then she laughed, the irony of the low brow bar circuit not escaping her. She was a tough-looking girl, with short, punkish bleached hair and strong muscles, so I was not surprised when she explained that she was considering moving into competitive body-building, and away from dancing. 'I've seen girls not making enough money dancing and becoming strippers, and I don't think it's for me. I'd rather be waitressing.'

'A lot of girls I know would rather not be doing it,' admitted Karen. 'The ones who've been doing it a long time – some of them have got children – are one-parent families, and they feel it's the best thing they can do. There's one girl I think of in particular who's got a daughter and she says it's good because in the daytime she's there with her child and in the night-time when the child's asleep she's at work. She feels she's still giving her daughter the same attention as she would if she didn't have to work, whereas if she had a daytime job not only would she not have as much money to spend on her little girl, but also she wouldn't see her.'

Stripping can be a risky occupation, though, for any young woman. Things can easily go wrong or get out of hand, with a funny or, more usually, less than funny result. 'On my second ever job the comedian who doubles as compere put the wrong tape in when I was about to go out there and totally threw me, but I still carried on and did the strip to the music. Dressed up as a Red Indian, I went out there to the Stray Cats playing "What's New Pussy-Cat"! About my third or fourth time after that – it was a big place called Tiffany's in Bedford, and it was an afternoon job – there was a big catwalk, with about four hundred men in there and I had my back to the audience. I was bending over, leaning on a chair on stage, and I turned round and there was this guy on the stage with his trousers and his pants round his ankles just above me. I panicked and told him to go away – that was sort of what I said to him! – and he said, "Okay, I'll just pull up my trousers." He went to pull them up and then he dropped them again and made a lunge at me, and I screamed and pushed him off the stage with his trousers round his ankles. He went off the catwalk, flat on his back, and the bouncers had to carry him out and take him to hospital with a broken ankle. That was quite fun.

'Another time I'd been in a show where the whole audience was fighting, and myself and another, drunk, girl who I had to look after climbed out of a toilet window in our leotards – as we were about to go on at the end of our act – dragging all our kit with us. There was chairs and glasses and everything flying.

'Another time I made the mistake – I didn't know any better at the time – of doing a river-boat on the Thames. Never ever do a river-boat that's not moored permanently. You can't get off. And this one was for Millwall Football Club, and I didn't realise it until I was on there and in the middle of the river. Suddenly they all decided to have a fight – there was not a stick of furniture left on the boat, it all went over. We were hiding in the captain's little space underneath the console for safety, otherwise I don't know what might have happened. Finally we got into the side and the police were there. A few times when that sort of thing has happened we've had to run out and leave our wages.

'I've got really mixed views on this,' said Karen. I had asked whether she felt devalued by her work, stripping off before a crowd of leering men, and was surprised, perhaps naïvely, by her response – after all, women do go into this business to make money. 'I had a conversation recently with a friend of mine, a girl who does striptease, and said I had to turn down loads of work. I still do, because people just won't pay what I want to do it, and yes I've lost out, and some girls will say that it's better to earn fifty quid than nothing. But my attitude is, if I go there and somebody calls me a cheap slag or throws any other insult at me about being cheap, I feel cheap, I feel like I'm there being paid less than what I'm worth. If I'm paid the minimum even of what I think I'm worth to be there then whatever they throw at me, it's water off a duck's back. I know that I'm laughing all the way to the bank; if I feel like I'm not, I feel like I'm a comedian, like I'm having the piss taken out of me.

'You see, I've been doing it longer than a lot of the comedians I work for and it really annoys me, it's so unfair the way our wages are structured – it never used to be like that. Often you also have a comedian who comes and does half an hour's stand up spot either in the first or second half of the show. Nine times out of ten they arrive at the beginning of the show and they say to the compère, "Quick, quick, get me on – I've got another job to do, I'm doubling." They have no regard for us, they don't ask us if we mind. They are usually paid between a hundred and a hundred and twenty pounds – sometimes around ninety – but I'd say on average about a hundred pounds they make to be there for half an hour. And when they've finished they sell their tapes at three or four pounds a go, so we all have to wait while they sell them. There can be one of them in the first and in the second half, and we're on our seventy pounds to be there all night.

'At the end of the evening we're sometimes asked to do a double act, which is a simulated lesbian double act, and to do that we're paid extra.' Later she explained that this double act usually consisted of the two girls writhing up and down each other's partly clothed bodies, with a lot of kissing of faces, arms and breasts, whilst gradually removing each others clothes, until they would leave the stage breathless, sweaty and naked. 'Either the organisers come and say, "Here is the money

30

from the club funds", or if it's someone getting married the best man comes. We do usually get paid on the spot for what we've done, though not always, but if we do our double act then they have to pay extra. It's not usually included in the price and often we have to go around and do a collection – in other words go round with a hat, which is illegal. It's begging, it's degrading, it gives the men a chance to grope you. Whereas in the past before we had pound coins if you heard a clang everyone would turn round and make fun of the man – so you'd make at least a pound from everyone. So about twelve years ago my wages would be about a hundred pounds a night – I expected to earn double my fifty basic. Now girls are lucky if they're earning eighty or ninety pounds a night twelve years later.

'Our money's gone down, everyone else's money's gone up. On a good night, though, you could earn a lot of money, like a hundred and fifty pounds, if you had a good audience and they all put in well. But some nights you won't get a double act. There's no guarantee that you'll get asked to do one, there's no guarantee that there'll be enough men there to put in. There's no guarantee that the men who are there are going to put in a reasonable amount, and for myself, like I said before, I have a price, and if they don't put in that amount I just don't do it. I say, "Here's the money, you give it to charity. I'm not doing it, this is my price." And I've fallen out with some of the other girls over this, because of course it needs two of you to do a double act, so if one of you says, "I'm not doing it for that amount of money", then the other girl will say, "Well, let's do a very short spot", and I'll say no.

You don't need to even know the other girl, or to have rehearsed, to do the lesbian double act. 'Some of us do, that's why some of us stick to our money. There's a few of us who do have set acts and stick rigidly to our money, but sometimes you may never have seen the other girl. But there is the basic way you always do it that all the girls know. Anyway, you can always busk it. But the business of money with the double act, it started off as extra tip money outside show time. In other words, if a show ended at eleven o'clock then at one minute past eleven you'd go out there with your hat, jug, whatever, to do your collection, so the show had to have finished on time. Out of that money you took out ten per cent and gave it to the compère because he'd have to still be there with his PA system for the music and to introduce you and take your things.

'Now what happens is that most of the shows don't have two guest comedians, only one in the first half, and if the compère has run out of jokes in the second half he'll kick you out there to do your collection within show time, but still expect his ten per cent. They'll kick you out there at any cost, or tell you how much you're going to earn to do the double act. The organiser might go to the comedian and say, "Here's fifty quid – can you get the girls to do a double act, twenty-five quid each?" So he'll come and say, "Right, here's fifty quid. You're doing the double act", and a lot of the girls will just say, "Oh yeh, okay then." If they come in and say it to me I say, "Sod off, I don't tell you how much money you're earning – where's the organiser? I'll tell him how much money I want to do it, you won't tell him."

'But it's unfortunate, it's just one of those things, it's like all of the sex industry – in this country striptease is only more or less legal, and prostitution isn't legal at all – if these things were to be brought out into the open and they weren't illegal then you wouldn't have pimps, you wouldn't have men running the show, women would be able to control it more. But all the while it's like this, swept under the carpet, nobody realising all these things are happening. It is total exploitation, it really is. It's very different from how it was when I started.'

I wondered whether it had changed over the years or whether the incessant strain of the work had changed Karen. 'I think it's a bit of everything. As I've got older my tolerance of men and my patience have worn thin. I've become more hardened to it but I also think men's attitudes have changed much more. Twelve years ago striptease was less risqué than it is now. Another example is the modelling I used to do earlier on. I used to do the calendars and everything, and Page 3. As soon as I took my knickers off and did a BBC thing nude, Page 3 wouldn't have me any more. As soon as they found out I'd done striptease they wouldn't have me. Now that would not be the case. You get all the girls who do the *Sunday Sport* and that, which wasn't around then, they're all doing men's magazines. Some of them are doing porno stuff abroad – I've seen it, I go abroad, I recognise them – so it's different, it's all changed now. The men, I think, expect a lot more – they're not happy, a lot of them, with just a basic striptease. How much further can you go? Even the girls who are doing 'blue', you can only go so far, and then what? How much more? Turn yourself inside out or something?

Karen persisted that it was the money that was the most important thing, though she has failed to set up a strippers' union because most of the girls wouldn't stick to a minimum rate. She is angry that they are not treated fairly. 'The money aspect of it really aggravates me. We always have it thrown at us from the comedians: "Ah, but you have the double act and the whip-round at the end." And I always throw back at them: "We don't, it's not a guarantee and for every good one we have there's another ten that aren't good or where we don't get a double act." They only remember the good ones, and also, by the time it's our turn the guys have paid out and paid out, and when we come to do our whip-round they say, "Oh well, I've already bought two tapes and raffle tickets, and I've paid to come in here and you're asking me for more money, bitch!" '

'That is sometimes the attitude you get from them. I hate it, I hate the whip-round, it's the worst bit of it. You just have to close your ears to the insults, though of course you care. But it's not always like that. Often they are men who are just insecure themselves, and they just don't know how to speak to women. It's probably why in all the years I've been doing it I've never ever been out with anyone from any of my shows – if you think of how many men I must have met in twelve years, and I've never ever been inspired to have a comedian or a punter as a boyfriend, never.'

To me it seemed sad that Karen had seen so much of the ugly side of men. She was constantly putting herself in a position where she was in a sense the victim in a crowd of leering, jeering, excited men. Always operating under the threat of the situation getting out of hand, of rape. Though she claims to feel a sense of power over these men as she performs her striptease, it is clearly a tense relationship, a precarious balance between control and anarchy. I wondered how she had managed to have any good relationships with men at all, and to what extent her experience had affected her private life. 'I don't think it has,' she insisted. 'Somebody once said to me, a friend, she said that when I dance I always have this expression on my face that's very hard to describe. She said it was almost sort of nondescript, like I'm looking at everybody at once. That's the only way she could describe it and I thought about what she said. I'd never really noticed it before, and I think what it is, is that when you're doing striptease you literally have to have eyes up your arse, you're looking everywhere, and when I'm in a club if I'm dancing, not working, just out enjoying myself, I do tend to be looking everywhere still.

'I suppose I'm much more aware of men. I don't like men to be over-affectionate with me too quickly if I don't know them. I'm not necessarily talking about boyfriends – it could just be men, friends of girlfriends of mine. We could just be laughing, having a joke about something, and they go to give you a cuddle or a squeeze – I don't like men to be affectionate unless they've earned my affection. It's just a switch in my mind that reminds me of men who are trying to grope me when I'm at work, which is sad, if you've got someone who's showing genuine affection, because unless I think they've earned my affection I don't give it.

'Having said that, when I'm in a relationship with somebody I am very affectionate. I don't think my job has stopped me or held me back in my relationships, not so much in what I do as in the hours I work – I could have been a nurse and had the same problems, working Friday nights, Saturday nights. I made a deal with Bob that I wouldn't work Saturdays so that we'd always have the weekends with each other, we'd always have one night we could go out together for a whole evening, and Sunday. I don't do Sunday lunchtimes any more. The only exception to that is if I have a belly-dancing job, which I love doing anyway. That's a real enjoyment for me, and if it's in London then he'll come with me and we'll make an evening of it. But with the actual striptease I try and stick now to Monday to Friday.'

Karen's work as a stripper is a valid freelance business; she is not like dominatrix Lindi St Clair, who was taken to court for non-payment of tax. 'I have an accountant and I submit tax returns. They tell me how much I owe them and I pay it, and the same with the National Insurance stamp every week. The TV companies I work for, and films I do as well, usually deduct National Insurance before they pay, and those things I'm supposed to add up and send the slips off to the Inland Revenue and then they'll refund it to me. So I pay it out every week and then they send a cheque back, which is really daft, but I never get round to it anyway, so they probably owe me quite a lot of money by now!'

Her success as a stripper extends to appearances in film and television. 'The last film I did was called *Split Second* and it stars Rutger Hauer who does the Guinness adverts. Ian Dury was also in it. It's a futuristic film, supernatural, and Rutger Hauer is a detective – it's a bit like *Blade Runner*. It's set in London in the year 2020, and the Thames has flooded, and they go into a night-club which has all these very weird, unusual people in it, and I'm the striptease wearing a rubber costume, with a mask on and all sorts of things, and I do a striptease for Rutger Hauer. I've also done three Ken Russell films. The last one I did was a bit of a cameo part in a film called *Prisoners of Honour*. I did *Salome's Last Dance*, and I belly-danced in that as well, and I did a small bit in a film called *The Lair of the White Worm*. On TV, last week I was on 'Hale and Pace', and a small bit in 'Beadle's About' is coming up. Basically I just do whatever work comes along.

'I'm happy to work in these films, but I'm very funny about doing men's magazines. I don't like opening my legs and I never do – I don't think anyone can afford to pay me what I'd want to do that. I think it's total exploitation – about a hundred and fifty quid a day most of the girls get to do the magazines. Well, on a good night doing striptease I could earn that, and definitely on two nights I could earn it without anyone taking a photo of me. They don't allow it. I mean, people know I do it, but it's not there in celluloid.'

Many of the women I spoke to had clear ideas about what they would or wouldn't do in terms of sexual work. I had always felt that there must be a moment when you made a conscious decision to break through the 'nice girls don't do it' taboo, but clearly there is not. Most women who exploit their bodies for financial gain never really breach that taboo in their own minds. The distinction between what you see as acceptable and what isn't varies with the work.

Karen expounded her own view: 'I do do nude photos, but I don't do open-leg stuff. I'm not against it. My boyfriend has a whole collection of *Fiesta* and that, and I enjoy reading them as well. I've got no objections to that, and I've got no objections to prostitution, but I wouldn't want to be a prostitute. I have no objections to the photographs, but I just wouldn't want to do it. I wouldn't want my parents to see it, and I don't think the girls are paid enough to do it. Most of the girls are there one minute and gone the next, only a few are kept on regularly. I just wouldn't feel happy. Then again I know other girls who do the magazines, who are very happy to do them but who can't cope with doing striptease – it's just not for them. Everybody's different, it's very personal when you're doing something to do with sex as a woman – more so than as a man.

'I think everyone has their level. If you were an Arab woman I suppose it would be just showing your eyes. For most women wearing normal clothes, wearing a low-cut dress would be daring – topless on the beach on holiday is about their limit. Then you've got the girls who take it one stage further, like me, and the girls who do the magazines, right up to the women who do formal prostitution. They've all got a level. Even a prostitute's got a level. As I understand it, they wouldn't kiss their clients, they've all got a set rate, and that's what they stick to. There's no question about it. Whereas men – male strippers or men in the sex industry – are looked upon completely differently. They're macho. The men envy them, I suppose, and I think they gain rather than lose status in the eyes of other men, and if they're powerful then they gain status from women as well.'

36

Having said that she finds it hard to trust men, and that she feels that women lose status by being involved in sex work, Karen might find Bob's obvious interest in other women, his collection of pornographic magazines, disturbing. But not so: 'I feel very secure with him, that he loves me. He likes looking at beautiful things. If he sees a woman and there's something beautiful about her he'll look at it. I can't deny him that and it doesn't upset me because I know he loves me. If I was to come home and find him with another woman, that would be different, I'd be very upset. But touch wood I don't think I ever will!

'I have had problems with boyfriends, though, mainly due to the hours I work, which I've now sorted out. I did have a boyfriend a couple of years ago who hated what I did. But I stopped stripping for a couple of years then and I only started again towards the end of our relationship, which was on the turn by then anyway. I had to start again because I needed some money and I wasn't getting any modelling work at that stage. Apart from that, with all the boyfriends I've had I've always been up front about what I've done, and they've either liked it or they haven't. If they've chosen to let it be a problem then in my eyes they weren't worth having anyway. I couldn't hide that part of my life.

'A friend of mine I worked with the other night, a stripper, she's got two children – one's seven and one's eight – and she was saying that the children have asked questions about things. Like they've seen the clothes she uses for work and know she works in the evening. And she's told them, never completely kept it a secret from them, but she's waited for them to ask. I thought: What would I do if I had children? Even if I'd stopped striptease, I don't think I would hide it from them, because I wouldn't want anyone else to tell them because that would make it seem even worse. I'm very protective of children, and I don't think you should allow them to grow up too quickly, and there's some things that they can't understand to start off with.

'By the same token I would never want to hide what I've done, I would never want my children to be ashamed of their bodies. I'm quite open like that – nudity to me is not a big taboo thing. I'll pass that on if I have children. I don't have any yet, but I would try and tell them at a young enough age that it would be a normal thing, that that was something mummy did before and those are pictures of mummy when she was modelling. And she hasn't got her clothes on, but so what? I wouldn't want it to be a big taboo thing.'

With friends in all walks of life, including 'the industry', Karen fits easily into society as she chooses. Those that may not approve can be ignored. 'Some of my friends have got jobs they call "normal jobs" – like a social worker, and another friend's a secretary, one's a shop assistant, and a very close friend of mine is a travel agent. They're all different and they all think that what I do must be really exciting because when I'm at a club mid-week I don't have to get up the next day. Then I say to them, "But when you're tucked in at night I'm on my way to work." It works both ways. They think it's very glamorous until they come with me to one of the shows and realise it's quite boring really, sitting around waiting in between going on. But most of them say they like my performance when they watch it.

'My best friend now does striptease, though much more part-time than I do, just because she has other work commitments, but she started because of me. She'd been my friend for some time and she came with me to a few jobs and then came to me and said, "Well, I'd like to have a go at doing that. Will you help me get a costume together and show me what to do?" So I did. She would have still been my friend if she hadn't been doing it. Mostly, though, I meet friends through the clubs I go to, and the one I help my boyfriend run, and they come from all different backgrounds.'

From my own rather limited dancing experience, which I gave up at the age of twenty-four, I assumed that Karen's career must change with age. 'Yes, it does. For the girls who do the circuit that I do, who are straight striptease, earning the seventy to eighty pounds a night, it's not so much how old you are as how old you look. As long as your body is good you can still carry on. Most girls tend to stop on that circuit when they get to their early thirties, but some of the girls who do stronger stuff go on to much older. The girls who are doing stronger stuff are either women who were working as gogo-dancers in the Sixties (who must be in their forties now, and they've kept going all the way through, having gone through the whole scene) or have started with normal striptease and as they've got older, perhaps had a few kids, they're not getting booked – their bodies aren't quite as good – and so they just do stronger to still get the bookings.'

When I inquired what the 'stronger stuff' was, Karen was not reticent. 'They'll do a vibrator show or they might give one of the guys a wank, oral sex, and in some cases full sex. Having said that, there are a few coming on the scene now who are young and quite pretty. Usually they come down to London from up north. They're just girls who come because they've got nothing up there – no work, no hope. They come to London and meet the wrong person in the industry who tells them that this is what striptease is about, this is what you have to do. They don't know any different, until they get put on a show with somebody like me or the girls I work with who say, "What are you doing? You're too young and pretty to be doing this, you don't have to do that, you can earn the same money without doing that."

'But by then they've got known for being what we call "blue striptease", and it's very hard once the girls have done that to then get booked on straight shows. Once the agents know you'll do that they'll push you to do it, so they can get more bookings. I don't know if they actually get more money out of it, it's just more bookings. If they can say to the client you can have two pretty girls who'll just come and do striptease and a simulated lesbian act and it'll cost you this amount, or you can have two pretty girls who'll come and do striptease, a simulated lesbian act and they'll do extras for the audience and it will cost you the same, or they'll go round with a jug at the end to do the extras like we would go round with a jug to do the double act, obviously they'll go for the extras. I mean, they're men, they'll go for the most they can get.'

Women are not in a position of power. 'Most of the agents are men. All the ones I work for are men – there are a couple of women agents, but not many. It's a very male-orientated business. Most of the people who book the shows are men as well, which I suppose is obvious. It's a funny thing, I've often thought of having my own agency – though now I'm turning my attention to my own shop – but I don't know how far you'd get as a woman, especially a woman who everyone knows has been a stripper. They wouldn't take you seriously and they wouldn't like it – they definitely wouldn't like it.

'It's a very old-fashioned set-up. A lot of the comedians expect some of the girls to not only be booked to do the show but also to give them a form of perks for booking them. And some of the girls are stupid enough to do it. I don't want to make myself sound like an angel here because I'm not, but as far as striptease goes I am. I've never got involved with anyone in that business, never sexually – I've always just done my job and that is it. I've always stood up for what I believe in, so I've made quite a few enemies. It's not the sort of business, really, where a woman can stand up and do that. It's not like being a woman in an office where you can jump up and say, "Sexual harrassment!" You can't do that when you're a stripper. The comedians will come in – not all of them but some of them – and grab hold of you and grope you and feel it's their divine right because you're there as a stripper. You have to get changed in front of them and not mind them wanting to touch you, and I do mind.'

In her private relationships, Karen had never thought to worry about her status, about how men would think of her when she became a stripper, mainly because when she started in the business she was living with a boyfriend who didn't mind. 'I ended up buying a house with him, and I stayed with him for five or six years. When I was eighteen I thought I was going to spend the rest of my life with him, I thought I had my man. When I broke up with him – which had nothing to do with my work, he had no hang-ups about that at all (he thought that men were mad to pay me to take my clothes off when he knew that on a good night with a few drinks in a night-club I'd do it anyway) – I didn't have another boyfriend for two years and as I was getting older the thought did cross my mind: Will someone want to marry me? But then underneath I always knew there'd be someone. I think there's someone for everyone. I knew I'd have a lot to give when I found someone, and then I did find someone. The only thing that did worry me was that I might not have found my someone while I was still of childbearing age.

'But it was all right. I think being a stripper has made me much more finicky, fussy, about my man. The man I'm with, Bob, is very, very tolerant. When I lost my brother last year he was a pillar of strength. I've not been an easy person to live with in the last year, for all sorts of reasons, and he's been so understanding and sensitive and he makes me laugh as well. His sensitivity is his best quality, unlike most men I meet, so if I find a man – not just my boyfriend, any man – who is sensitive to a woman's feelings, it really means a lot to me because I don't find many men who are genuinely sensitive and sincere. At work I don't see a sensitive side to the men at all.

'All the comedians, ninety-nine per cent anyway, tell racist jokes and are very, very racist. They didn't like it at all when Bob came along. When he came with me on a couple of jobs and word got round, their whole attitude towards me changed, and it was after that as well that I made the stand about the money and everything. But I know it was mostly because of Bob. Not that he's ever said anything to any of them – he never gets involved in my work – it's just the fact that he's black. They've got their own ideas, you know, black man living with a stripper . . . Apart from that they just don't like black men, full stop. Especially of course because he had gone where none of them had managed to go before and he was black.'

However much she would prefer it not to be, her status continues to be a pressing factor when it comes to the practical issues in life. 'I've found that because of the work that I do, when I've had to do serious business I've often been looked down on. Things like buying a house – they don't necessarily know what I do, but I don't necessarily have to spell it out. They can sometimes tell what you do, especially if they know you're working evenings – they might think I'm a hostess or some such – and then there's my attitude, the way I speak to them. I don't take any shit from them at all. I have been referred to as "girl" in a proper business deal, when buying something serious. The man will say, "Well girl, it's like this . . .", and that really aggravates me. When you're discussing buying an eighty-thousand-pound flat you do not refer to me as girl!

'Apart from that, I don't really know whether people look at me differently because I take my clothes off for a living, because I've been doing it for so long – since I was eighteen – and I've always been extremely open about my sexuality, I've always worn what I wanted to wear, I've always said what I feel, and I've always done what I've wanted to do sexually. I don't have any inhibitions, I really don't. So if a man is looking down his nose at me, I'll usually come up with some very choice lines, depending on what he's said to me. Or I won't bother to say anything at all – sometimes men like that aren't worth the breath.

'It's like if somebody is racist through and through, it doesn't matter what you say to them, you're not going to convince them any other way. They might even believe that they could change the way they feel, but the moment they had a row with a black person he would be a black bastard as far as they were concerned. If you've got a man who is sexist in this way, even if he doesn't show this side of him to his woman, if he's that way inclined as soon as he had a row with you you would still be "bitch". You can't change men's ingrained attitudes that have been there for centuries. Some things have changed over the last twenty years, but not everything. You can't change everything. Anyway, it's because it's a taboo subject that men will pay to see you strip in the first place.'

Karen plans to give up stripping and open a fantasy clothing shop, her way of keeping involved in an industry which allows her to express her sexuality but does not expose her to exploitation by men. This theme shop, which she is hoping to open soon, would give her the opportunity to shape her life as she wishes it. 'The shop's going to be in Camden [North London], it's called Libido. Bob is opening a club called Libido as well. The idea is that it's a dance club with sexy clothing, not that you'd have to dress up to go in. In all the other clubs you have to dress in leather, rubber, PVC or catsuits to go in – in this one we'll be taking it a bit more broadly into fantasy. It'll consist of all kinds of rave gear that you could wear. Maybe you'd have a pair of leggings on with a rubber strip down the side and a pair of trainers and a costume top or something, sort of sexy but ravy at the same time. I knew Bob wanted to do this club and he kept saying, "Wouldn't it be great if someone opened a shop that sold the right type of clothes?" Because no one place does it, they're either very fetishy or very ravy but there isn't a cross-over. You have to go all over London to get a bit here and a bit there.

'Then a friend approached me who used to work at a place called Atom Age, and at Skin Two in West London, both places that sold fetish clothing. She said she wasn't working there any more and needed something to do. I said I needed something else to do too, I was fed up with striptease, and that's how it started. I love going to the clubs, and I've been involved helping Bob. I've known the friend for a few years and selling this sort of clothing is what she knows best. We both like wearing it as well, so we're not selling something that we're not into doing, and the whole thing is like a concept – you'll be able to buy tickets for the club at the shop. I've got lots of contacts and so does she. It'll be useful for girls doing striptease – a lot of the things we'll be selling will be good as costumes.

'I'll still keep the belly-dancing going if I'm asked, because I enjoy it. I'm a member of the Middle Eastern Dance Association. I've also started writing. I've written for a women's magazine which is going to be launched soon. It's a sex magazine for women which they say is for the middle shelf. I've given them a short story and three sample episodes of a column they asked me to write. It's a sort of bitchy but sexy column about life from a woman's point of view, like my own diary.'

I am struck by Karen's energy for life, her infectious interest in sex and her enjoyment of her own sexuality. She sits beside me in the pub drinking her Britvic lemonade as the evening wears on, full of plans for the future. I wonder how she feels now about the twelve years she has spent in striptease. 'It has been a positive thing, because I feel the striptease has given me experience in life that I can now pass on, write about. Not only experience with men, but with women who I've met professionally. Their experiences with men and all of that is worth remembering.'

4

The men have always got to be virile

'Women can feel powerful in themselves. If you've got any sexual charisma at all you feel you have power over men up to a point.' I'd first met Paula, a hard-core porno-film star in her early forties, at an exhibition of her erotic paintings at a Pimlico gallery having been taken along to the opening by a television producer I'd worked with often who admired her work. Now I sat in her rented flat, above a village-like parade of shops in North London, one Sunday afternoon, drinking wine and chatting with both Paula and her live-in boyfriend, Frank. She looked such a demure person with her neat, dark bob, freshly scrubbed face, cream blouse and calf-length pleated skirt, that it was hard to connect the woman with her erotic landscapes, which were beautifully drawn but startlingly pornographic. The decor of her flat was 1930s suburban, in contrast to the complex personality she expressed as an artist and model.

'And so,' she continued, 'you see a lot of women using the men around them to get money out of them. I've seen lots of young models of nineteen, twenty, very attractive girls who are just using men and extracting enormous prices for a very minimum amount of co-operation. In a way, though, I feel sorry for them because they're using their attributes while they're still there, and you feel that once they're thirty or so they won't get so much attention. In the porn industry as a whole if you keep your hands on the reins, and choose what you want to do and don't allow them to make you do things you're not happy with, then you're all right. But I find that unless you keep a firm grip on it you can find you're losing your perspective and your direction.

'Some women have emerged stronger for it and some have not. I think it's always the case that if you can use your experience and make something out of it, then the moment you've had enough you can get on with something else. It's just sex, it isn't addictive, though some people have a high sex drive and some people have a low one. I've got a high sexual drive towards having adventures, towards the erotic. But I haven't got a very high sex drive at all, really – that's why I'm not a person who needs a huge amount of sex, but I do like adventures and I like erotic experimenting within safe circumstances. I've always been a bit worried about other women's attitudes towards me. I could be seen as being rather a threatening influence to married life in general because my ideas are subversive. I could be seen as an encouragement for people to go off and have affairs, to be free and not respect the marriage vows. But I myself don't wish to live within those confines.'

She had started as a nude model, she explained, only when she was thirty, at the beginning of the Eighties, but she has a Sixties attitude towards sex, left over from her teens. 'I don't think I was ever a proper hippy, though I think I would have liked to have been. But when I lived at home there was such a restricted atmosphere.' Paula's mother was a very dominant woman, the father quiet and under her thumb; Paula and her sisters were all very much influenced by their mother and her strongly held repressive views. The fact that Paula now lives with a much older man, Frank, probably has something to do with this family background.

Entry into the world of pornography 'was the culmination of a long series of things. It was as if I'd come to a time in my life where my work was running down, my interest was running down, my own life was hemmed in. I looked at it and I thought something needed to be moved – I was always saying no to everything. I was more and more isolated, working at home painting, working very hard and not getting paid much money for it. I don't know, it was just a bit of magical transformation – you know how you get driven from within. There are moving times in your life when you almost have to let your intuitive side take over.'

And, I ventured, all this was due to years of family repression? 'Totally, yes. I had no idea of the extent of it, really. But

I'd been in *Hair*, I'd taken my clothes off on stage and danced about and I thought I was quite liberated. I thought I was really laid-back and sexually liberated but actually I wasn't at all, I hadn't even begun to understand men or understand myself.

'I got myself tied up with the idea of religion. I thought that perhaps the best thing to do was to make myself utterly pure. I went religious and anorexic, a sort of spiritual anorexia as well. I thought that to be thoroughly pure inside, you had to cleanse yourself thoroughly of all the lusts and appetites. I was afraid of the feelings, of my appetites and of my own nature. Every now and then – it was like being schizophrenic – my pornographic side, my lustful side, would burst through if I got a bit drunk at a party or something. I knew another side to me existed in a funny sort of way – it used to burst out at odd moments and then I'd go back into my shell again. I'd had boyfriends, but always very short-term relationships with men. Usually only about three or four months, that was the extent, and I always knew it was going to fizzle out. I'd suddenly get fidgety and lose interest – it seemed to be a pattern that repeated itself. I didn't feel I was a lesbian, either. I just felt I'm not in charge of this.'

Paula never felt that she made a conscious decision to enter pornography as a 'world', in order to gain control of herself, although this is what it boiled down to. For her it was a gradual move. 'I saw an advert in a magazine and I decided that I would write off and do just a little bit of nude modelling – it's very tame really, nothing extraordinary. I couldn't have contemplated doing hard-core porn at that time, it would have been completely impossible for me. So I thought I'd just write off to the magazine and say I'd like to 'do some modelling because they were advertising for models. Then when I'd written the letter I thought: Oh no! I wish I hadn't now. I hoped they'd never reply anyway, but unfortunately they replied immediately and said, "Come along for the interview and we'll tell you about it."

'And I did, and it all happened surprisingly quickly. At the first modelling session I'd never been so terrified in my whole life, and I thought: Everybody must know what I'm going to do. I felt dreadful, appallingly dreadful, as if I was just about to murder somebody or do something thoroughly immoral, but when I got there all the fears melted away, and I thought: I'm born for this. I knew all the positions to get into, I knew the right sort of feelings to project – something in me just thoroughly responded and the other side of me came out. I loved it. Having done one session, I wasn't pressurised into anything, but I was offered other work, so I said yes, and then I couldn't wait. Every time a new session was coming up I used to look forward to it tremendously. I got very obsessed by it. I don't think many pictures appeared in this country, but mainly abroad, and it turned out the photographer was doing photographs for many different publications.'

Although this work didn't appear in England, I did wonder how her friends had felt about her new venture when she discussed it with them. 'I didn't have any girlfriends at that time, not really. I met girls in it, so, all on the same tack, we could talk about it. But mainly, to begin with, I only met amateurs, who just came in and did an odd session and then went home.'

These women were presumably doing an occasional modelling session mainly to make money, but for Paula it went very much deeper than straightforward financial considerations. 'Yes, there was the money. I needed the money at that point, I know I did, and it certainly came in handy. But it wasn't just that at all. There were some girls who were just modelling for the money, in which case they weren't getting what I was getting. It was just so nice, for somebody like me who was so scared of sex to be open about it, to meet people on the terms that we did, where we knew we were going to be safe. To start with I was just doing soft porn. Then I went on to do some hard-core stuff, which amazed me because I really liked it. It was still, at that point, fairly relaxed. If I hadn't wanted to do something, that was okay – it was to do with how well you get on with a person.

'But I did feel good, we all had such tremendous fun, and this was before Aids. Funnily enough, the photographer, who I liked very much, also worked with another girl who went through a similar metamorphosis as myself. She got herself very interested in the whole business and she used to take

48

photographs of couples screwing and then suddenly she'd drop the camera and leap in and get involved herself. And this was something that grabbed her for a few years and now she's gone back to being a wife and mother again, and being fairly conventional. There's something that some women feel they need, as opposed to the professional girls who model for *Penthouse* who often don't want to give any more than they have to give. I don't actually find that I get on so well with them – they're just exploiting their beautiful figures – but I suppose they're enjoying themselves too.

'I haven't actually met thoroughly miserable girls, who hate it. During the early days that I was doing it, it was just fun and not a great deal of money. Nobody was tricked into it, some of the girls were swingers [people who attended partner-swapping sex parties]. With swinging, it's usually the men who drag their reluctant wives along, but then often the wives end up more enthusiastic and carry on for far longer than the men. One woman, who kept saying, "Oh, my husband wanted me to do this", turned out to be the most lecherous and demanding person of the lot once she got into it, and the husband in a way was just following her demand for adventures.

'But that's never the way it sounds when the women tell the story. They don't like to take responsibility for their own lustfulness – they'd much rather say, "Oh, my husband forced me to do it." I've heard that so many times, and yet quite often once they're immersed in a swinging party they're the ones who get carried away with lust. And then they get rather worried about it, so they withdraw themselves because it's a little bit too difficult to cope with. I think we keep our marriages together sometimes by restricting them down a narrow path, and men don't like to think: What would my wife be like if she got turned on by another man? How many men would she want after that? Most women assume that husbands are lecherous, but husbands don't necessarily want to think their wives are – they want to think their wives only respond to them, can only love one person.'

Having talked with Paula about the strictness of her family background and her shy public personality, I felt that her first experience as a pornographic model must have involved a crisis, not just breaking through her private barriers but endangering her respectable role in society, her reputation. But this hadn't worried her.

'I thought: To hell with it, I want to do something that I can't deny, something that will put me completely out on a limb, because I want to acknowledge myself. I didn't think very much about reputation. I thought that, well, things weren't as bad as they used to be. Had it been fifty or sixty years ago it would have been different, but then, things were quite liberal at the end of the Seventies. The magazines were quite outrageous. Now they've gone back.

'I did tell my mother about it at the time. I made a point of telling her quite early on when I was doing fairly harmless things. I thought if anyone came across a photograph I'd hate her to have it from someone else. Imagine how horrible it would be for mum if she suddenly was confronted by a caring friend saying, "Well I thought you ought to know ..." So I thought I'd spare her that, she might as well know. And she was a bit bothered – well, very bothered – but it was an important part of freeing myself from her. She was always quite dominant, I didn't realise how much I was under her influence. I can't underestimate how much the modelling meant to me. It completely changed my life.'

It seemed strange to me that it took something that was anything but innocent for Paula to gain a sense of young innocence, a chance to be free of the constraints of her childhood.

'In the early part of doing it I was completely over the moon with what I'd discovered, and I suppose people saw me and thought: What a naïve, sweet, innocent child. Here she is, a thirty-year-old woman, acting as if she's fifteen and just discovered what it's all about. I think they were baffled by me and thought: How can you do this? You're completely uncorrupted by it. There's nothing sleazy about it, though. I thought it was so lovely. I realise that there were people who took advantage of it a bit – they thought: Oh, okay, she's enjoying herself. Lots of people would come in and take advantage of a girl who was willing to experiment. So I did, and I got in with one or two magazine editors who I wasn't terribly keen on. I didn't like what was going into the magazines very much. I didn't like the general philosophy behind it.

'The general magazines you see around, you read them, the ordinary sex magazines today, and there's nothing particularly offensive about them. But I used to hate the way the articles were written, the way they presented and described the girls. It comes from America – phrases like "porno sluts" – and using words like "scrubbers", and I really got very mad at those descriptions. I thought: Well, here I am, I'm actually giving men the fantasies that they say they want and they're going to insult me for it. I was mad at the men at that point for not coming forward and being honest about it themselves.

'It's all very well for men to say that women aren't honest about their lust, and one can understand why they're not, actually, because women have been labelled "bad girls" or "fallen women" for years. And I've read about Victorian women, prostitutes, and even a girl who got pregnant and, because she was a maid or something, had no way of supporting herself. She couldn't bring anyone to court, even if she'd been raped by her lord and master. I can understand if women are cagey now, because even if you are giving men what they say they want the tone in which they describe you really disillusions you.

'I was once given the chance to write a diary in a magazine and I thought that that was nice, because most of the mags don't use real women – men write instead. I wrote one article myself and the rest of the time it was done by a man. They took it away from me, and they published so-called interviews with me which were not. They published drawings of mine and things that I hadn't given my permission for, and I felt very unpowerful. It's not a nice feeling.'

Working in the sex business, Paula clearly has met men who she feels have exploited her. But she has also found that, because of what she does, she's had to tread carefully with the women she has encountered both through her work and socially.

'I've been very careful, and if they have had feelings of disapproval they haven't said so to me. I've been very wary of them. I've not had many close female friends for the last few years, but I'm getting more now. But I have had female friends within the same area, the people who I've worked with. We've understood each other perfectly well, and they've never seen a threat to their own boyfriends. It's a completely different sort of world, and if you know people who are swingers as well, they understand what the discipline is, whereas a person living a conventional life will misunderstand what you're trying to do. Sexual freedom always involves another person. It's all very well saying, "I am going to be sexually liberated!" If I'm going to be sexually liberated I'm going to involve other men, or other women, so it's never something which is just you doing it. You've got to always think about the other people you're involving. Anyway, that's one frightening thing.'

This understanding of sexual freedom and its implications for taking responsibility for the other people involved shows a side of Paula which I respect. She seems to be a person aware of her own feelings and able to analyse them. It was incongruous to imagine her in relation to the blatant insensitivity of pornographic films. 'Having been a professional actress myself, I assumed that a porn film would be properly scripted and filmed in the way that I would be accustomed to doing it. I thought: Well, at last I can use Frank here, because he's a writer. I can get him to write a script for me and we can actually do something new and different. I wanted very much in my first one to get some of the philosophy that I myself felt very passionately about. I wanted to act myself going through the experiences I'd just had and show what a marvellous effect it had had on me.

'I'd met a director in the course of my early modelling, and I'd heard about him having made quite good films in this country. I didn't give a thought to whether it was legal or not – I assumed it was, I suppose, because things were quite open. He was one of those old hippy types and he said, "If you want to put a message in, then do." I've talked about this many times, because it really makes me laugh now. There was a real spirit about it. We got a script done and we sent copies to the other artists in it, hoping that they were all going to turn up

52

on the day, having learnt their lines. And of course they hadn't, they hadn't even looked at it, and the one that had looked at it was scared stiff because she'd never acted before in her whole life. All she'd been was a model, really, so she was petrified.

'It was made over two days, and the script was not kept to at all, so what came out was far from what we'd intended. I was so disappointed. It did accomplish something, though. In fact, it got me quite well known. It got me in touch with a lot of other people who I was very pleased to meet, so it was a marvellous film in a way, but it wasn't what I planned. It got put into magazines as having four stars [highly recommended] – whatever that meant!

'The success of the film introduced me to a lot of interesting people, so I discovered a kind of alternative world. And the director, who was a pop singer, was a great person. We all became great friends and meet up still, ten years later, veterans. Before this porn work came along I'd been feeling very isolated, I hadn't met anybody. I'd met a few people in theatre because I was painting with people in theatre, but every contact I made I had to work hard at. And then suddenly I did this video and people just came to me in flocks – and they weren't just wankers, they were people in the arts and films and all kinds of things, interesting people.'

So, I asked, what did she do in this film? 'Everything,' Frank answered for her, and laughed a lot. 'Well,' said Paula, unruffled, picking up the story once the merriment had subsided, 'it was straightforward. It wasn't an S and M film – it was straightforward sex. It was the story of a repressed young girl meeting up with a curious guru type of man, who initiates her into a world of sexual experimentation and challenge. And it was trying to put into a nutshell some of the things I'd gone through. In fact, the story was about how they used to shake a dice to decide what to do. The second half of it was based on a thing that happened during the War when they would take you and drop you somewhere dressed in a full German uniform, and see if you could get back to headquarters without being caught. The guru chucked the girl out of the car, stark-naked in the middle of a very ordinary suburban district, and she had to get home. That was the idea behind it. He was a mysterious man who wanted somehow to train her to understand herself better, and she had to go through this slightly risky business of being dumped on the street without clothes, because they'd thrown the dice.

'Frank and I did this ourselves in our own private experiments years before. We used a dice to give us ideas. I felt so trapped in what I thought I wanted to do that I wanted fate to decide. So if you had an interesting idea you had to carry out the challenge, depending on how the dice fell. It was only small things, like going out with your coat on and no clothes underneath it, which is something I wouldn't bother to do now because it doesn't mean anything to me now. I'm not challenging myself now – I don't need to – but in those days I needed to challenge myself with those sorts of silly things.

'The whole point of the dice therapy was that you had six options and you must write down six, some that you knew you could do quite easily, like stay home and watch the sport on television. And then you'd got to challenge yourself to do something you wouldn't think of doing but might if you were challenged – things that you had a *frisson* about, slightly risqué but never dangerous things. And it damn near always came up on that. We never put down things like walk down the street stark-naked in front of the police station. That would have been stupid and you would have just got yourself into trouble. And I'd have never gone for a walk stark-naked on the common and lay myself open to being assaulted or anything like that. They were always very safe things, but things that made you feel slightly excited though also a little bit frightened for your own modesty. But compared to some friends of mine I was not at all outrageous, I still had barriers to break down.'

Paula had found the freedom of childhood, to dare to do naughty things. But she continued professionally in her quest to do pornographic film work that she considered meaningful.

'I did that first video and then nothing for about a year. Then the telephone started ringing and I met loads of people. I was introduced to pornographer Al Goldstein and I went to America, and I met a film producer as well. And somehow or other a film offer came through in the States. I heard a bit about the film and it sounded quite interesting. A man and his wife were working together as a team to make the film, and it had a script, which is one of the things that appealed to me about it. I received the script by post before I went so I could learn my lines, and the wife of the director was the writer, so it was a woman writing the script, and she got in some really good ideas.

'The film was definitely loaded on the side of women. It was called *Women at Play*, and was about a radical female director who goes and does a production about a set of women in Greenwich Village. This director is working them very hard through a series of sketches, and it's about how these women found out about their sexuality and developed themselves – rather in the way that I did. It was a sort of comedy, about the effect this had on the women's husbands and boyfriends. They were supposed to be ordinary girls taking part in an amateur production. I was playing the director, so I had quite a lot of nice things to say. I think it was a very unusual film for an American company to make. It didn't really have the usual themes that you expect to find in a film, which are there to flatter the men, so the men are usually seen "fucking their brains out", as they say. I used to hate that expression.'

Once again the film wasn't all she'd hoped for, though. 'In the end they still had to let the men have the last word – I was a bit let down by that. I did a few more films with that couple. I liked them very much and each one we did was better than the last, the scripts got better and better. And we used to talk quite a lot about the whole theme, and the script-writer eventually got rather fed up with the limitations. I'd keep on having similar sex scenes – you've got to be there and they've got to go a certain way, the men have always got to be seen to be terribly virile and wonderful. And also the men themselves, I found, were always wanting to give the impression of sex being a sort of assault, that they're there to pump away until the woman's screeching with pleasure. There was no gradual build-up to anything. It was all pump, pump, pump, a bit like American action films are – lots of action and car explosions.

'They didn't seem to know how to vary things. They'd employ six girls to be in the film, and several men, and they'd have scene after scene where the same thing was happening all the time with different girls. They didn't know how to show character in a person's sexual nature. They'd have a girl who was supposed to be very innocent coming in, her first experience, and then she'd be dashing in and the next minute she was on the job quite happily. There was no real thought given to trying to put any meaning into the scenes. If you ever mentioned the word "meaning" to anyone they'd just laugh at you.

'I mentioned to Al Goldstein once that I really would like to do a much more artistically viable film, and he said, "Oh, don't give me that pretentious crap." And I felt very let down by Al because I think it's a problem with semantics with the Americans – the word "artistic", to me it just means well done and creative, but to him it means arty-farty, pretentious, not erotic. They just think: Well, what's the point? This is just for a load of men to come and jerk off to. We don't want a lot of script and stuff. They're just going to fast-forward that till they get to the bit that they can jerk off to.

'In a way, I thought, I'm not against them jerking off if they want to. It's just that I'm not interested in doing just that because it's boring, thoroughly boring to watch and very boring to be in. So I made the decision that the very primitive straightforward porn, though I had no objection to it being there at all if people need it, is very limiting. You don't need big budgets to do it – you could do it in a garage.'

I'd met Al Goldstein myself, and could see what Paula meant. He is very much a straightforward businessman who has built up what could be termed a porno empire in New York by giving the punters exactly what they want, and no fussing about with meaning. The man himself seems to me to enjoy it all enormously. I first met him when we were staying at the same hotel in L.A. and he invited me to the Porno Oscars ceremony, at which he was to arrive as star attraction dressed as Count Dracula, and pop out of a coffin. Curious, I went. I felt the most remarkable thing about the evening was a table of male porno stars whom I watched as they waited to hear which of them would be the porno stud of the year. Clearly, it hinged not on who was the best actor, but on who could have and hold an erection at will. There was a mixture of nerves and amusement on their faces as they waited. When the announcement was made, the curly-haired young man who'd won bounded up out of his seat with excitement and relief, to whoops and cheers from his colleagues. This was what it was all about.

'To be honest,' continued Paula, 'I went through a phase before I started modelling myself where I wanted to see a porn film just for the sake of seeing one. So Frank took me to a club. I thought I'd be the only woman there and I'd feel awful, but it was fine. It was a little tiny porno club and I just watched all these films, which were good, bad and indifferent. Actually one was quite a good film and the rest were mediocre, and a bit obnoxious. But the overall effect for me was a tremendously liberating one – I just wanted to see the sex acts being done, so I could see how it was done properly.'

She wasn't embarrassed for long, when she first saw herself on the big screen having sex. 'Anyway, I was only watching it with the people in the film, and then once I'd got used to it I was quite happy to watch with other people, provided they liked it and weren't going to judge me for it or feel in any way upset or annoyed or disgusted by it. I wouldn't want to show it to anyone who was going to be disgusted by it. But at first I was a little bit shy about watching myself. But having seen the first film, I could see that I reflected the fact that I was enjoying it – if you know you're not, then it's painful to watch. There have been one or two things I've done where I know I was a bit bored, or a bit annoyed about the situation, like there was one where the script just went completely out of the window and my face looks completely bad-tempered. And there was one where I didn't get on with the man particularly well and I didn't like the director, and you can see it. But on the whole I enjoy watching them because they are usually well filmed. What I don't like, what does embarrass me, is when they film close-ups of the genitals, because it could be anybody. I don't mind seeing my face and my whole body, but whenever they show a close-up of that bit I feel just a bit not good.'

A puzzled journalist who went to interview Paula in her hotel room in New York, who she described as 'epitomising the clean all-American boy', asked her what a nice girl like her was doing making blue movies, pointing out, 'You're English, an actress, a well known painter. You talk like an educated lady.' She responded archly, 'I do it because I enjoy it. I do it because I'm not as nice as you think. Hardly anybody is! I do it because I'm a blatant exhibitionist.'

'For me,' she explained, 'performing sexual acts, not merely simulating them as in other forms of drama, taught me a lot of things about myself that I didn't know or suspect. It helped me to clear out those blockages caused by suppression and repression. I found that I was turned on by situations, fantasies and acts that nice girls are not supposed to know about, let alone like. I had to face it. I did like them. I was disgusted, fascinated and appalled, all at one and the same time. Unexpected desires of a bizarrely masochistic nature were simmering away in my mind and my imagination.'

Later she went on to make a film called *To Ride a Tiger*, in which she explored the limits of her own masochism. The film told the story of a young artist who went to Amsterdam to live out her dreams and become the heroine of a modern *Story of O*. The *Story of O*, by Pauline Réage, is an erotic literary classic of exquisite sado-masochism. It is a story of male sexual control and woman's total submission and use in sex games. Paula felt wonderful after making the film, despite the fact that she suffered bruises for weeks, and was asked to fly to San Francisco to lecture on sexual deviation. She didn't go. 'Life is too short to have myself reduced to Freudian jargon and intellectual gobbledegook.' But for the most part she feels that the genre of the porno film has failed her. She would like these films to be about exploring the many aspects of sexual fact, fantasy and desire, and they are quite clearly not. Mainly they are made to fulfil a basic need and to make money for the backers and distributors.

Paula had started out as a non-pornographic actress working for the most part on the stage in the provinces. It seemed a pity that she hadn't kept this up, since it was more likely she would have got meaningful scripts outside pornography. 'When I was twenty-five I decided I wouldn't do any more acting, mainly because I felt that my talent was greater in fine art and that I wasn't getting where I wanted to go in the theatre. I felt I was limited as an actress, and now I look back I can see why, because my sexual side was so tied up that I was an enclosed person. And if I could see any of my early performances I think I'd see that I wasn't projecting outwards at all. I knew I wasn't getting very far with my acting. I had quite a lot of nice jobs and I always thought: After this the phone is going to ring, this will be my breakthrough. But it never was. I think one of the reasons was that I looked so young. When I was twenty-five I looked fourteen, partly because of my hairstyle – long hair with a fringe – it looked very teenage but I wouldn't cut it off.

I smiled. I also had long, dark youthful hair I didn't want to cut. As I sat there with Frank playing with my baby son in their living-room that afternoon, it all did in a way feel innocent. Paula in her demure blouse and skirt, the sun streaming through the window – at a glance it seemed not at all probable that she was a pornographic actress. But she has managed to liberate herself by giving full vent to the extreme contrasts in her character. 'Acting in the theatre at the start of my career did begin to bring me out of my shy self, I did become quite an exhibitionist on stage. And it was the same with my repressed sexuality. I needed to take my clothes off in public for magazines and in films in order to release my sexual self.'

5

Pissed on four Babychams

'I was once in a porno film where I had to wrestle in jelly,'
began the tall, glamorous, now former, editor of *Penthouse*,
with more than a glint of humour in her eye. The jelly had
unfortunately not set, and Linzi Drew and her co-wrestler
found themselves immersed in a watery mush. Unperturbed,
she suggested someone go to the local supermarket and buy
the sort of oat bran flakes her brother had for breakfast, to
thicken it up. Chocolate bran flakes were soon added to the
pool – with the result that it was impossible to see any of the
women's bodies, 'let alone open-leg shots. Covered in the stuff,
we fell about laughing.'

For all her raunchy past, Linzi Drew comes across as an
efficient magazine editor with a lively sense of humour. In her
early thirties, over the last ten years she has worked her way
up in the pornographic magazine business from pin-up to
journalist to editor. We met in her last summer as editor of
Penthouse. When I rang her at her home in Surrey she suggested that, since she had several meetings in West London
and I had a young child, she should drop by to see me. My
neighbour answered the door to her, as she had rung the wrong
bell. He stood open-mouthed, surveying her from her four-inch
red stilettos and tanned legs to her black skin-tight halter
mini-dress under little red jacket and her long, peroxide-blonde
hair. Linzi is not the sort of person you'd expect to find on
your doorstep every day. Once inside, she was friendly and
candid.

'I am editor of *Penthouse*, but I get all the nice parts of the
job really. I do some of my writing work at home, and because
Penthouse had really good PR when I joined, I do all sorts of
radio and telly stuff. I've just brought my own video out and
I went away to do this American book on porn stars. You

know, if you get a little bit known people ask you to do other things, which is good for *Penthouse* and good for me. So I tend to be doing lots of things. People always link me with the name *Penthouse*, so if I'm doing any PR work it's good for *Penthouse*.

'I got started when I was about twenty, about twelve years ago. I was working in an office, and I was rather bored. I also worked as a barmaid for Bristol City Football Club. They were in the First Division then, and they decided to do promotions on the pitch when they had big crowds coming in, so we got a cheer-leading team together called the Rocking Robins. I was a cheer-leader and we got a lot of coverage in the national press. The *Sun* and the *Star* and that sent photographers down, and we also got on the credits of 'Match of the Day' because we happened to be in a televised match. We were called the Rocking Robins because of that pop song. We had these awful silver boots and paper pom-poms – not a very expensive outfit! And from that national coverage came the modelling. A few of the photographers said to me, "You should do some modelling, love", or something as daft, and I thought: Well, it beats working for a tobacco company weighing out vouchers, which was very boring, and you were next to the factory which was pretty smelly anyway. I don't smoke so it seemed silly. I thought I might as well have a go at that – it had to be better than what I was doing.

'Basically I got some photographers to take some pictures of me and I sent them off to some London model agents and got accepted by one, the Geoff Wootton Model Agency, and so I got a flat in London and moved up there. That sounds very easy, but it wasn't actually – getting a flat in London wasn't. Moving from living with my mum and dad to coming up to London was quite a big step for me, and finding a flat, and then when you first start modelling you don't always get much work.'

Linzi began work as a 'glamour' model, doing underwear and topless calendars. She then went on to work for a porno-graphic magazine called *Club International* as a nude model, revelling in the work. She recalls with amusement doing her first striptease. When it was discovered, at a party her magazine was holding on a river-boat, that the stripper had missed the boat, Linzi sprang forward and began to dance and throw her clothes off. She was a huge success. When her boyfriend came to pick her up she had sheepishly to admit she'd done the strip, but fortunately he knew her well enough not to mind.

'I was the first real person in the men's magazines. All the others were faceless – you know, "This is Fiona from so-and-so and she likes skin-diving." So people started writing in to me and it really worked, as it did with Fiona Richmond all those years ago. I did a series for four years, which was ten pages every month for *Club International*, before I worked for *Penthouse*. It was a selection of pictures with a sort of diary alongside. I'd write one sexy bit in it – like, if I went to a party and I saw something sexy happening. Then I'd write what I'd been doing with work – if I did a TV show where I was playing a stripper, and something funny happened, I'd mention it. And if something particularly funny didn't happen that month I'd go back and say something about the last month, or say, "That reminds me of a fantasy of mine . . ." Basically it was a two-thousand-word piece with pictures inset and letters if the punters wrote in to me, and with my replies. I'd also do other promotions and features for the magazine, so I got a big following with the readers.'

Linzi didn't think much of the other models, 'all those models who do Page 3 and all that. They think it's fine to be getting their boobs out on Page 3, but you know, they won't show any other bits of their body. They say, "I'll show this bit but not this bit", which I think is really daft. If you're standing up there to be looked at by men, the guys are going to have a wank over you whether you're showing your boobs, your bum or what. I always think it's a bit ridiculous to say, "Oh no, I wouldn't show this bit or that bit."

'Then *Penthouse* were having a staff change-around at the same time that I'd made a video, which has been released now, called *I Love Linzi*. It was about the ups and downs of a model, me at a photo session, me at a strip job. A couple of friends of mine were in it too – it was just like the *Electric Blue* video. And a journalist from *Penthouse* came to interview me and said, "We're having a change-around at *Penthouse*. I'll mention that you're looking around for something." The next day *Penthouse* rang me up and said, "Would you like to come and have a meeting with us?" So I went along and took my sack of letters from *Club International* – I used to get hundreds and hundreds. And so I went in and said, "Look at these, it seems to work, but I'm looking for a change." And they said, "We're having a meeting in a few days and we'll get back to you." They rang me in a few days and said, "We'd like to make you our editor on a three-month trial."

'Obviously it was a bit of a PR thing, but working with Isabel Kaprowski it really did work, and I've been there for four years now and my job at *Penthouse* is very promotional – a lot of PR, which pulls in advertising. If I go to the Motor Show and meet people at the Kenwood stand and get friendly with them, then they ring up and put a lot of advertising our way. So my job is a funny sort of job. I'm in the office and I'm at the editorial meetings saying what's going to go in the magazine, but I'm not going to be in the office five days a week like a normal editor is. I'm the one who gets invited to premières and parties, which is great for me. It's worked really well.

'When I first joined *Penthouse* I was doing the same type of thing – photos, and writing about what I'd been up to every month. But then about a year and a half ago we decided to stop that, and I only do photo sessions for the magazine every now and then. The last one I did was in February. I was on the cover and did a feature.' She giggled, commenting that in fact it's much quicker to use nineteen-year-old models who don't need as much careful lighting as she now does at the decrepit age of thirty-three. 'I just have my letters page now, with all the letters that people send in. And I write different pieces in the magazine, but a lot comes in from America because we pay to use the American name. And basically my job is different from week to week.'

But what exactly does she feel she is promoting, in the PR part of her job? There are many people who campaign against the kind of work she does. 'When I'm up against the Campaign against Pornography people, they always say that the business I'm in is sleazy and degrading, and I say, "Well, I don't feel

I'm degraded, I don't feel demeaned." I've felt that I've made a career out of something when I probably wouldn't have had one – well, I probably wouldn't have had my own business or anything. I don't know what I'd be doing, but I'm very happy in the career I've chosen.

'These people say to me, "Well, you're not typical, you're just lucky really. It just happens that you're not typical of the sort of women who usually get involved in pornography." But I think these people who are against pornography really don't know much about it. They come up with statements like "The sort of women you show in *Penthouse* are being dominated, you'll see them tied up, you'll see them with shoes near their pussy." Or, you know, they say that there's frightening imagery in magazines like *Penthouse*. I think that very few of them actually see magazines like *Penthouse*. They think there's all sorts of things in them that aren't in them. We can't show things like women holding implements that look like they're being pushed up inside themselves because we're not allowed to. We're not allowed to show two girls together, we're not allowed to show any form of bondage whatsoever.'

Gesticulating widely, Linzi enthused over her profession – a startling and vivid presence, her long, painted nails skimming my sofa as she sold the idea of the work she believes so strongly in. She argued firmly against the critics and for the virtues of porn. I was reminded of something performer Paula had said: 'Porn does not kill love. It isn't about love. It is about sex. Nothing more and certainly nothing less. It deals with sex in every other form than love and marriage.' Paula had made the point that porn, unlike glamour and erotica, does not lie, but 'it has been made the scapegoat for deeper evils we do not care to examine . . . mostly, porn is too trivial to evoke all this anger and debate.'

'They talk about all the magazines,' Linzi continued more calmly, 'from your *Razzle* magazine, which is a sort of cheap and cheerful one, to *Penthouse*, which is the most expensive glossy biggest one, as having the same frightening, disturbing images in them. There're not frightening, disturbing images – they're just pictures of women looking lovely with no clothes on. And if they find that frightening and disturbing – well,

I'm sorry, but I don't. I think sex is something that is enjoyable and pleasant, and reading about it in a magazine should be normal. Our stories are heterosexual – a man and a woman making love, just general fantasy stuff. And our features are about people like Sean Connery, interviewed this month, and Bruce Willis last month, and Cher. All those sort of things would appeal to men *and* women.'

I queried that the magazine was intended to appeal to both men and women. 'It's just the pictures. And we can't really do anything about the pictures because the laws in this country say you can't feature men with the women. American *Penthouse* and other American magazines show couples making love. We're always criticised for showing women on their own, so depicting them as sex objects. I'd like to see magazines made legal where you can see men and women together, but you can't do that, you can't get distribution – that's why the magazines are full of photographs of just women. Men would still buy the magazines and women would buy them too.

'This doesn't include the pictures in the really down-market mags that get very small distribution – they won't get distributed by Menzies or Smiths, which gets you two hundred thousand sales. If you put guys in the mags as well, you're at the low end of the market that just gets sold in corner shops. Most of those magazines have cheap printing quality, and the photography's awful; if the nearest thing to a camera is someone's foot, you'll get the depth of field and everything incorrect. I'm not saying that *Penthouse* should change, but it would be nice if other quality magazines, with photographs for men and women, were available.'

Linzi's working class family were not particularly disturbed by the way she has chosen to earn a living. 'They were fine about it. When I was twenty I did my first magazine photographs, which were for *Penthouse*. So I told them. I said, "Oh, I've got this job this afternoon for this magazine." My dad was never a reader of *Penthouse* or anything like that, but he just said, "Oh yeah? Great, love", and didn't take much notice of it. And then, when my pictures were out in the magazine and one of the neighbours said something to him, he said, "I didn't know you were doing that sort of thing." I said, "I did tell you, and yes, I am going to do that sort of thing. I don't think there's anything wrong with it, and I hope you don't mind." Since then he's been okay. I never show him the magazines I appear in, or my columns. I think he'd be a bit shocked if he did see them. When I do my letters page in *Penthouse* I like to make it as rude as possible, because the guys like to read it rude, and I find it nice to be raunchy for them. I like the letters to be raunchy, I like doing a slow build-up. There are certain words I don't like using in the magazine, ones that I think are horrible, but if someone writes a letter in and they use certain words, I think: Shall I change it? Then I think no, I'd better leave it in because that's the word they wanted to use. I enjoy what I do.'

Though she has a happy and stable private life now, living with her musician/porno-film-maker boyfriend, in the past Linzi has experienced clashes between her work and her private life. She explained about one particular occasion when she had problems with a man. 'It was when I first started modelling. I went to the States, to Los Angeles, and I was only going to stay two weeks, but I really liked it and so I wanted to stay for six weeks, but I didn't have enough money. So, I was walking along the street, and this guy came up to me and said, "You should do some modelling. Can I take some pictures of you?" So I thought I'd do some modelling and earn some money. He took some pictures of me and sent them off to *Hustler* magazine. *Hustler* is an American magazine with a big three-page pull-out in the centre, which is like *Playboy* but slightly ruder. American magazines are always a bit ruder any-way; but *Hustler*'s a good-quality magazine, just quite raunchy.

'So I did *Hustler* magazine. While I was over there I had an American boyfriend, and when I told him I was doing *Hustler* magazine he absolutely flipped and disappeared. He went absolutely crazy, and said, "You're not doing that!" I said, "Well, I'm only here because I model." I suppose he didn't know I was going to do *Hustler* magazine, but I wanted to stay in America and I wanted to earn some money. I didn't want to ring my mum and dad and ask them to lend me five hundred pounds so that I could stay. I wanted to stay in

66

America without asking someone to give me some money. So that's what I decided to do and I thought: Well, if that's what he thinks then I can't be doing with it. Because I don't really want anyone telling me what to do – I want to be able to do what I want to do. And since then I've had boyfriends who actually like what I do. If I'm doing some writing and it's raunchy and I get off on it, then they get the benefit of it too. I've never really had a boyfriend who would say, "I don't want you to be doing this, I don't want you doing that", because I wouldn't be with somebody like that.

'I suppose if I told someone, "I'm in a porno movie and I'm having sex with three men in it", then they could possibly say to me, "Well, I don't want you to." If you're actually having sex with somebody in a movie then you've got all the Aids-type problems – it's having a relationship, in a way, with someone. But if you're just posing for pictures and things like that it's not the same.'

Linzi did, however, change her *Penthouse* diary articles to suit the changing climate. 'Now I don't write about myself as being promiscuous. If someone writes a letter about a particular sexual experience I might reply saying, "Oh, I remember when I screwed in the back of a bus with a boyfriend of mine." I would never write, "Well, I remember going out and picking up three guys and fucking them in the back of their car" – I would never say that now. But I would say, "Well, I remember when me and a boyfriend had a wonderful fuck in some location" – you would actually say it as "me and my boyfriend" or "my boyfriend of the time", or something. And also I'll say, "I went to a party. It was a bring-a-bottle-and-a-condom party." So safe sex is referred to, and, the way I speak to the punters who write to me has changed. I do tone that down. I can still make it naughty, without saying I did it with fifteen men in three weeks. Now I can say I did it with the same man but in fifteen different positions!'

In general she finds that people outside the pornography business are not openly shocked by what she does. 'But I went to the Milton Keynes pop festival a couple of weeks ago and some guy in a band came up to me and asked me something about my cut-off denims, and then later he came up to me and said, "My friend's just told me who you are. I'm really appalled!" That was the first time anyone had said that to me, and I said, "Oh, are you? Sorry about that" in a surprised way, and after that he carried on talking to me.

'I suppose, where I go out for enjoyment in my private life most people either don't know who I am so I don't get to speak to them, or I already know them. I went to a party at the Grosvenor House Hotel recently and I was put on a table with people I didn't know, and they said, "What do you do for a living?" I said, "I'm the editor of *Penthouse* magazine", and the ladies seemed very interested. One was a social worker and another a hospital administrator. *Penthouse* seems to be the acceptable face of pornography. Wherever I go in the world, if I say I'm the editor of *Penthouse* people immediately know what it is and want to talk about it. They look at me and say, "Are you a model?" I say, "Well, yeah, I do sometimes still model for the magazine." If I say *Club International* people say, "Oh, what sort of magazine's that?"

'I remember I was once doing something for Central TV and I was going up to Birmingham with Isabel Kaprowski who was the editor of *Forum* then, and Adam Cole who is the editor of *Electric Blue* magazine. We sat next to each other on the train, and there was one space opposite us in which a lady was sitting. We were talking about the show and about the figures – we had to refute the anti-porn people's linking them to sex crimes [figures gleaned from the 1990 government sponsored Howatt and Cumberbatch report]. Also, we had some figures about the other European Community countries where hardcore pornography is legal. And after we'd been speaking for about five minutes this lady got up and said, "I just can't sit here any more, and you two are women! I can't believe that you work for a magazine like that – I think it's completely disgusting." And she picked up her coat and stood up. She just wouldn't sit down in the same carriage as us.

'Men have always been looking at the naked female form in some way or other because of the way a woman's body is. It is a very attractive thing to look at and I don't think there's anything wrong with that. If I see a woman walking down the street and she's got a lovely pair of legs, or lovely blonde hair all down her back, or something, I would like to be able to say, "Hasn't she got lovely hair?" or "Hasn't she got a lovely figure?" But if men say things like that about women these days, other women get shocked and say the men are sexist pigs and they shouldn't do that. And I don't see why, if you look at something and it's pleasing to the eye, it's so wrong to say so.

'I'm a feminist, I think women should have equal opportunities. If women want to, and can, become directors of companies, or if they want to become plumbers, or if they want to appear naked in a magazine, I think they should be able to do that. I don't think some women have a right to say this is wrong and pass their judgements on what other women do. Women should have the right to decide whether they're going to use their brains, or their brains and their beauty, to make a career for themselves. I think you use what you've got, and that's what I've done, really.'

Linzi hasn't got time for people who think models lack status. 'I don't think by taking off your clothes you change yourself at all. We all take off our clothes at some point, and if you take them off as a job then that's what you've decided to do. I do think that if someone decides to do it they've got to actually enjoy it. People say that a lot of the girls are forced into it, that they don't like it. I get tons of letters from girls who want to do it – they think it's a great career, they want to be Page 3 girls, they want to appear in *Penthouse*. It's a glamorous business. You couldn't appear on Page 3 or in *Penthouse* if you looked like you hated every minute of it. You've got to be relaxed and enjoy what you're doing.

'When I first started modelling I didn't know whether I'd be able to do it or not. But I just thought: If I do it and I don't like it then I won't carry on – it's not like prostitution where people get into it and get used to the money, or need drugs, so they carry on. Modelling is not very easy to get into. You've got to be quite keen, because you've got to get a model agent, you've got to go for castings. You might go to six castings and not get any jobs, so you've got to be pretty dedicated to do it. You can't just say, "Right, I'm going to be a model", and the work floods in, because it doesn't, it's not that easy. So people who do it, do it because they want to do it. No one is forced into it.'

She explained how it all works. 'Generally, if you've got a casting, you take a portfolio, and you show them the portfolio. The problem with that is it could have old pictures. I've booked girls for things and they've turned up and not been right for the job. One girl in particular, I saw her photographs and she looked fine. We booked her, and she'd had her boobs made smaller. I don't know what the operation is, exactly, but when someone has their boobs made smaller it looks like they've moved the nipples, and on this girl it looked awful, very noticeable. It looked like they'd taken her nipples off and sewn them back on. In her portfolio she looked fine, so you wouldn't know.

'So generally at a casting you take your portfolio, and if a photographer is particularly interested in using you, taking you on a trip abroad or something, which costs quite a lot of money, they would then say, "Can you do three polaroids?" And you'd then take your clothes off, probably keep your knickers on, because that's okay, or probably you'd take a G-string. Then they do a back view, a front view and a close-up of you – just one for their record and one so they can see that you haven't had anything done to your body since you had the other photographs done. People are always having things done to their bodies now. When I was in America, everyone in the business was having their boobs done.'

There has always been plenty of competition in the modelling world. Despite her stunning appearance, it wasn't all easy going for Linzi when she first started. 'Castings are usually all right, though it can be a bit like a cattle-call. When I used to go for calendar auditions when I first started modelling, you'd get every model in London turning up – a hundred and fifty models and they'd only want six – and you'd think: God, that was a waste of time! But you go, because you might get that really good calendar. So sometimes you spend ages getting ready, you go all the way across London, and they look at your book for about a minute and a half and say, "Thank you, next please." But that's the modelling business all over, really.'

How must it have felt when she went on her first modelling jobs? The only thing I could conjure up from my past to compare it with was when, as a graduate first starting out, whilst writing a play I worked part-time as a life model for an art college. I distinctly remembered the nerves I suffered on my first session in a cold studio, and the embarrassment before I got used to it. Even then, I didn't stick it for very long. Though I enjoyed meeting the artists and seeing their work, I knew I had to look for a different job to pay the rent.

'I was a little bit nervous,' Linzi confirmed. 'The first shots were topless ones, and then a photographer asked me to do some nude pictures. But when you first go to the agencies they send you to see some of the photographers they know, who will take some test photographs for the girls so that they will have a starter portfolio of work to show. And as well as doing photos for the girls, if they do some topless pictures and they can sell them to any of the tabloids or *Titbits* or those sorts of magazines, then they get the money back for their film and their time, and they're always looking for new girls for possible jobs.

'So I went to a photographer who was round the corner from the agent I'd been to see. You don't have to pay for that – you do it because he gives you a bunch of pictures afterwards. You might choose twelve pictures, and he's got the rest to sell around the world, to syndicate. These would only be topless pictures – you wouldn't do nude for that. He'd pay for all the film, which is fairly expensive. If he shoots ten rolls of film it's going to cost him a hundred quid, and his time, so he has the privilege of selling the pictures for you. You can then get him to do some prints for your portfolio, which is what I did. And then that photographer asked me to do some nude pictures. He was quite nice – I was comfortable working with him – so I did and it was quite Okay because I'd done the topless pictures before.

'The first thing when you're modelling is that you wonder if you look a twit. You get into some position, and you feel insecure – you know, do I look daft in this position? But the

71

photographer's going round saying, "Oh lovely!", "Hold that, smashing!", "Oh great, lovely!" They give you confidence. If you get one of these photographers who says, "Oh I'm not sure about that shot", then you lose confidence. So photographers are very rarely like that. They're always saying, "Great, hold that, oh yeah, just a bit, great, wonderful!" So you don't feel that you look silly.'

The girl who now runs the show came up through the ranks, with panache, and fought hard for her success. Linzi thought back to the first modelling session she did. 'It was fine. I drove round to the studio in Fulham – I lived in Clapham then. I bought a four-pack of Babycham, and I sat in my car and drank it before I went in to do the shoot, to give me a bit of Dutch courage. I don't think you can really get pissed on four Babychams, but it seemed to help.

'After that time it became much easier. I went on a trip abroad, to Senegal, West Africa, which was the next set of pictures I did, and lying naked on a beach seemed a bit more natural than being in a studio. I went with seven French people, which was quite difficult because the French like to speak French and I didn't learn French terribly well at school – I passed my O-level in it, but couldn't converse! So it was a lonely two weeks, though it was in a lovely location in a Club Med hotel and I got really well looked after. But I wish I'd worked more – I only worked for three days and the rest of the time I just sat around not doing anything. But I thought that if I'd been on a trip with people I could speak to it would have been much nicer, which it was when I went on other trips. From there on in I got better work and it was okay – you just get used to it, I suppose.'

Linzi Drew has come a long way since that first job. Now she makes a far from silly impression, speaking honestly and with conviction. She is a successful career woman in what is still really a socially unacceptable field for women. She feels strongly that women should publish pornographic material and, equally, as consumers, have the right to be turned on. When I spoke to her recently she told me about the book she has just written for Virgin, *Linzi Drew's Pleasure Guide*, and

72

about two videos she has been in which will rival the *Electric Blue* video.

She's also about to launch a new adult education programme on satellite television, which will mean getting up to interview guests from the sex world at approximately 2 am. And, utilising her broad experience of life, she has written her first novel. Her success has not prevented her, though, from finding herself up against the authorities in an obscenity trial. As we talk, she expresses the hope that the Budget of the following day will eclipse her in the press, and that she'll be able to take up her new post as editor of *Men's Letters*, a magazine which is to be part of the Portland Publishing group which publishes titles such as *Penthouse* and *Forum*.

6

A bloody good way to earn a living

'I think the laws surrounding prostitution interfere in a way that they shouldn't in this day and age. The laws encapsulate a very nineteenth-century attitude to women which shouldn't prevail. But on the other hand, I do think that prostitutes are their own worst enemy; the laws are still there because prostitutes buy the notions of prostitution that are held in society,' complained former prostitute Helen Buckingham.

'Prostitutes share the mores of the society they live in, and if the mores of that society say prostitution is bad, then the people who are constrained through some set of circumstances or another to follow that way of life feel it is bad. They feel bad about themselves doing it and will go to extraordinary lengths to hide it. And they do exaggerate what will happen to them and project that inner social disgust outward. They'll say, "It will kill my mother, the children will laugh at my children at school, the press will flaunt pictures of me everywhere, the police will raid me, my neighbours will point fingers at me." They over-exaggerate it, so they don't tell, and so the police will say, "There goes one of those paranoid little so-and-sos. She's not going to stand up for herself – we can have her." That's how it feeds back to them: "I'm a victim, you can walk on me." '

Helen, tall and gaunt with large glasses framing her serious face, sat primly in her quiet Hampstead flat. Neatly dressed in an autumn-leaf-coloured track-suit, her rather lank black hair in a neat bob, some sewing in her hands, she reminded me faintly of a middle-aged aunt I'd always been fond of who used to lecture on Classics for the Open University, and would go for brisk walks in the country, dressed in comfortable tweeds. It was hard to imagine Helen, now in her late forties, working as a prostitute. But, she insisted, she had always been open about it.

Prostitution had rescued her, as a single parent in the Sixties, from a terrible poverty trap. 'My child simply grew up with it. His experience was: "Oh, the kids at school's mothers have seen you in the papers and they want to meet you for tea!" So you don't actually get all the strife that they say you'll get. You get people, especially women, being incredibly interested to meet you. And they're fascinated but not particularly judgemental. Or, they're trying to see themselves in your shoes – "What would *I* do?"'

'It's not judgemental or nasty, and certainly the police wouldn't come anywhere near me, because if they did they would be in the newspapers the next day.' One of the first prostitutes to come bravely out into the limelight to address the issue of prostitution through the media, Helen has been an articulate force in challenging conventional views and victimisation. She has always encouraged women to stand up for themselves. 'I've never had any trouble from the police. If I've had any trouble I've gone to the police, and they have always come on to my side. Their attitude depends on how you view your situation. If you say, "I'm not in the wrong – he was", and you go to the police with that attitude, they will buy the attitude that you come with. They will tend to take your side. After all, they're men of the world too, they've seen enough of it.'

But since soliciting is illegal, though being a prostitute in itself is not, if the police catch you soliciting they will presumably have to do something about it. Helen pressed her point: 'If you're one of the victims, they'll say, "Right, this is another statistic for us tonight – we can probably fuck her down in the cells too", because you're giving out those signals. But with me they would probably be very loath to caution me, very loath, because they would say, "Well, this one goes to the *Mirror* and tells them that she's been cautioned." And they don't want a lot of journalists poking around and asking a lot of questions about how they're carrying out their duty.'

One of the things that Helen has found interesting is that people often assume that it is prostitution that damages people, whereas she feels that in fact it is the other way round: it is damaged people who tend to go into prostitution. 'I think an awful lot of trouble is brought on by the paranoia that exists in people who have been abused.'

It has taken great courage to make herself into a recognisable media figure over the years, with her regular comments in the press and appearances on television and radio. 'It's been found over and over again in other countries that the only people who can actually make a dent in the situation are the ex-prostitutes. They are no longer living in fear, they've matured a lot, they've been through it all, they're the ones who will talk to the MPs and the police and the judges and the ones who can go on television and be laid-back about it and speak fluently. People who are actually on the game are far too nervous and far too excitable to be able to have serious talks.

'Usually prostitutes will go on television in black masks, which frightens viewers. Nothing puts you off more than someone speaking to you from behind the shadows in a mask. Immediately people think there must be something very wrong with them. Nobody wants to identify with something dark and shadowy and smacking of crime. So it's no good trying to get people to talk from behind masks – it just makes matters worse. The awful thing is that you put off the people who don't know you, but you don't fool the people who do know you. So if it's going to kill your mother, your mother's going to see it and be killed. She's going to know it's your silhouette, she's going to know at once. The person you want to protect is not going to be protected and the people you want to get through to are going to just have this barrier up.'

Helen had told her mother at an early stage. 'My family were so mad that I didn't think I had anything to lose. They were so good at fooling themselves that if they didn't want to know they'd tell themselves it wasn't true. I didn't really mind by then. They were no support to me in life anyway, so I couldn't see what I owed them. I didn't see why I had to keep quiet in case it killed them.

'I have sisters – they didn't go mad when I told them what I was doing. Most people don't. Some men do. Some friends of mine have been caught out on television. When brothers and fathers go bananas, mothers and sisters usually say, "Well, I don't blame you, dear. You didn't have much choice, did you? I'd have done the same in your circumstances." ' This seemed to me a terrible and desperately sad statement, family members turning their backs on their own, unwilling to help. The statistic quoted by the English Collective of Prostitutes, that seventy per cent of prostitutes are single parents, came strongly to mind.

Though born in London, Helen grew up in the country, in the south of England, in a middle-class, puritanical and repressive family. She fled up to London as soon as she was old enough to leave home, and threw herself into the fun-loving sexual spirit of the Sixties. But it wasn't long before she fell in love with a rogue, who abandoned her as soon as she became pregnant.

For her, the moral leap into prostitution had not been much of an issue. 'In the Sixties we were jumping in and out of bed with all and sundry anyway, so that kind of taboo had already gone. But the thing that worried me the most was whether I deserved the money, whether I ought to be paid for this, whether I was giving good service. How did one professionalise this, what was it really supposed to be about? I couldn't believe that it was so easy to get money for jam.'

Surely it wasn't as meaningless or as simple as 'money for jam'? The idea of going out on to the streets and picking up men or even meeting men in bars might, justifiably, give rise to fears for personal safety. 'I suppose the first couple of times I wasn't frightened that anyone would do me any harm, but I was frightened that I would not be able to tolerate them, because I think women are brought up with a tremendous sense of revulsion against men in general. And then there's this over-romantic idea of the one in particular they're going to end up with. I know a lot of women have said to me, "Oh, how do you stand it? It must be so disgusting and horrible." And yet when they've tried one, some have said, "Well, let me try one of yours", and I've said, "Well, okay, you go and fornicate with him and see." And they've come out and said, "Do you know, it was really nice. I didn't mind at all."

'I mean, this is money for jam, it's extraordinary how easy it is. It's not changed my relationship to men, it's just the same. In fact, it's slightly more honest.'

77

Interestingly, she found that in the Sixties it was the with-it young men who were horrified by what she was doing. 'I challenged the current supposition that men could have women when they felt like it, with no obligation, and that women enjoyed the sex, enjoyed giving themselves, enjoyed being walked over, enjoyed being used, enjoyed being disposed of. They thought that this is all part of the feminine personality: women are masochistic by nature and they like this. And to meet a woman who said, "No, I'm not like that and I don't like it, but this is a bloody good way to earn a living" was terribly, terribly threatening. Not to older men who've learnt the ways of the world – they realise that if they want any kind of sexuality later on in life that they can call their own, then they have to come to some arrangement with the female sex. That is something that men learn as they go along, but when they're young and romantic I think they don't care.'

She had been speedily disillusioned by her short flirtation with free love when her boyfriend had left her, pregnant. She was on her own at a time when abortion was still illegal, and facing a life as an unsupported single parent. There was little provision for childcare at the time, and she was forced to struggle along for some years on inadequate Social Security payments.

'I was very happy when I first worked as a prostitute, because suddenly all the pressure was off. There was money about, I could meet the bills, I could have a few of the things that other people in society have – like a television set for a start. Just a few things like that – I could have a telephone, I could take my child on holiday, I could buy clothes, I could pay the rent.

'I was about twenty-three when I had my son, on my own, but I was thirty before I realised there was such a thing as going on the game. I brought up a child on my own for six or seven years before I went on the game. It was very hard work. It was horrific, absolutely horrific. There was no help whatsoever at that time. You couldn't even qualify for a council flat because you weren't a man. You were hounded by Social Security, who wanted to have you totally isolated from your friends, especially from men, but what it amounted to was being isolated from women too. You were meant to live in total isolation where the only person who was supposed to have access to you was the Social Security officer.

'They did spy on you, they did follow you and they did come and inquire if they saw anybody coming to your house. They did go through your wardrobe and see if you'd bought anything new, and they did come and interview you on a very regular basis so that you had to learn to hide things. I kept special raggedy clothes that I'd had for ten years, to wear when they came round, so that they couldn't say, "You've had new shoes since I was last here." You weren't supposed to have had new shoes. And if I'd acquired anything from a tip or skip or something, like a new chair, I'd always hide it round at the neighbours'. I made big preparations for when these people came to visit. I'd look around saying, "My God, is there anything I shouldn't have?" – even just a simple thing like a pair of scissors I'd bought for my sewing. They'd look around saying, "Well, you didn't have those last week", so I'd have to hide them.

'For a long time I scraped a bit of a living doing dress-making, but it really was a bit of a living because clothes were pretty cheap in the Sixties. The off-the-peg things were very cheap, and the whole idea of going to a dress-maker was to get them even cheaper. People always bought their odd bits in the sales and they always wanted you to fit a three-metre dress into a two-and-a-half-metre piece, and they thought because they were doing it on the cheap your labour ought to be cheap. So it really was scraping by. It just helped meet the cost of ordinary things that Social Security didn't meet. There was no luxury about my life at that time at all.'

Becoming a prostitute meant that she could meet men who didn't use her in the way that other men in her life had. She was able to turn her back on these unscrupulous boyfriends and concentrate on herself.

'When I went on the game I found I was meeting a much nicer class of man, a really nice man. And I thought: Why should I put up with all these arrogant chauvinist pig bastards for nothing, and get into trouble with the Social Security if they find out that I've seen one of them? Why put up with this? This is sheer misery. I started by working in a night-club, and it was so nice to meet people without any front, people who were just straight forward. They got out their cheque-books or their wallets, didn't moralise, didn't want you to sacrifice your whole life to them, didn't want you to admire them and tell them how wonderful they were, didn't want you to be in love with them and didn't want to take up any more of your time. So I was infinitely better off.'

Helen thinks that things have improved a great deal for women over the last twenty-five years, particularly in regard to rights at work to equal pay, maternity leave, and the general accept-ance in society of lone parenting. In the early Sixties, she felt, the general ethos was very much against women who were independent. 'But on the other hand they owed sex to every-body, including themselves. That idea had got into the current ethos – it had escaped from the avant-garde psychoanalytic circles. The Freudian ethos was about, the great Sixties liberty was in, and we were supposed to be joining men on equal terms to participate in this. But actually the laws surrounding women's position hadn't changed at all. Of course, they had to in the Seventies, but in the Sixties they hadn't. There was no room for illegitimate babies.'

A sharp edge of bitterness pervades her description of life as a young single mother in the Sixties, and to some extent her account of her descent into prostitution, when she would perhaps have preferred help with childcare and a job. Instead, there was only disapproval.

'There was no legal abortion yet, and no room for illegitim-ate babies, no room for single mothers. There just was no provision whatsoever – certainly no nurseries or crèches or anything like that, just a few extremely seedy baby-minding establishments which were Dickensian. So that got me very angry. I'd had a university-geared education, I'd been told women were equal with men, but I could see that no way were women equal with men, no way. Of course, you then find anyway that having studied for this, that and the other, women aren't allowed to actually do it. That didn't change till 1976 [The Sex Discrimination Act], so you think: Well, what on earth did they tell you all this rubbish for? So I don't think anybody I met felt they were damaged by prostitution. They felt that they were rescued through it, they salvaged something of their lives through it. That's certainly the feeling I had about it.'

Helen didn't mind the sex itself, but I still wondered about the element of danger. Had she had any bad experiences with men? 'No, I had fewer bad experiences with men as clients than I've ever had with men in my private life. I think that men, when they have to pay, show considerably more respect. I mean, men live with and through money, they judge things by money, and if they can have it for free it can't be worth much – that's always been the case. And I expect men to fork out, because otherwise they don't respect you, they really don't – because they have to pay for everything else. They don't have as much to offer as they think they do. One is geared to thinking that perhaps one does need them, but apart from sex and money there is not a lot men have to offer.'

Clearly, Helen doesn't like men very much. Sadly disillusioned with them so early in her independent life, she has never married. Hostility towards men, coupled with an almost aggressive independence, substitute for a permanent relationship. But had this outwardly calm, friendly, and frequently funny woman (especially when entertaining me with comic imitations in a high pitched cockney drawl of prostitutes talking about men after work) living in her clean, airy flat, now with her second fatherless child, ever wanted to be married? 'I've lived with lots of men, and nearly married several, but when it's disintegrated at the end of the day I've realised that I'm actually better off without them and that with them my life has been quite severely curtailed. I have usually ended up propping them up, with their problems and all the rest of it. And if they're not able to provide – and many of them nowadays don't see why they should – what else have they got? Why should you want to be a mental nurse, a childminder and a general dogsbody for nothing? If you're not getting anything back, any emotional input back, any spiritual input back, and often not even much in the way of a sexual input back, what do you want it for?

81

'Most of us found that we had more of a status as prostitutes, although we weren't supposed to say so, than when we were just being single mothers – though most prostitutes continue to have men in their life and it continues to be a mess. It's unusual for a prostitute to have a happy marriage, because even if she has drifted into prostitution to save a marriage, which is often the case, when the husband finds out what she's doing, he doesn't like it. It does more harm to men than it does to women, I think. There were a lot of married women on the game who didn't tell their husbands what they were doing, but it had a very disruptive effect on their marriages.'

She denies the commonly held assumption that prostitution itself puts women off sex. 'On the contrary, it turns them on to sex more than ever, which is why they want a man in their private life to have their kind of sex, because they're not usually having their kind of sex with a client – they're making sure he has his kind of sex, though sometimes these can coincide. So much of prostitution is to do with kinky sex, which is what *he* wants. You're just setting the scene for him to have good sex. But the prostitutes are always looking for someone to provide their sex.

'For women this sex is tied up with more of a romantic thing, but for a man it seems to be, very often, a macho thing, he will think: "I've got this one, this one and that one – I take the money from this one to spend on that one." It always seems to end up on that kind of level. Or the husband doesn't want his business got back on to a viable footing if a wife in prostitution is the price he has to pay for it. He doesn't want the money coming from that source. So it's either lies or stress.'

Over the years Helen has worked in most areas of prostitution. 'I've worked in an escort agency – in fact, I've worked in more or less everything except street-walking. All of these things are down to what your personality is best adapted to. A lot of women say they wouldn't do anything but street-walking, because they like to see what they're getting, they like the freedom of not having any kind of boss at all – night-club staff telling you how to sit, where to sit, what to wear, what to drink, and all that. They just find it easier. It also depends on locality. There are still some parts of English cities, not so much London but some of the northern cities, where there is a lot of mateyness out in the streets still. A lot of northern women have grown up being used to the street as a place where you can be, whereas in London you think of it as a place you want to get away from as quickly as possible. You only go into the street to get a bus or a taxi or do some shopping. For some women in the smaller cities or neighbourhoods, they're used to the neighbourhood access and they feel at home there.'

Pimps can be a liability. 'Sometimes the men tend to come along to make sure their woman's all right, or to warn that the police are coming, but that can often turn into a heavy type of bully who comes along to make sure she earns enough money at night. Then if you go into all that with women, you find that it does tend to be a lot up to you whether you're going to have a heavy pimp round your neck or not. An awful lot of women will put up with relationships with men which involve a lot of bullying. Especially prostitutes. I'm particularly surprised that prostitutes will put up with it, because they're not married to these people. They don't have to put up with it.

'They'll say there are all sorts of psychological guns at their heads and I suppose that there are, given the fact that most women who come into prostitution tend to have had a long history of abuse and disaster in their lives, or they're the sort that have had a short, sharp crisis which means that they can't pick their lives up again. Given that so many are used to abuse all through their childhood, they take abuse to be the norm. There's not a lot the police or any of us can do about it.'

Helen has always had far too much self-respect to tolerate pimps. 'I certainly wouldn't put up with downright bullying. No man's ever hit me. I've never got involved with that kind of man. Certainly, I've had all the usual problems that women get with men – that they're feckless and fickle, moody and difficult; they want you but they can't afford to keep you, and if you try to support yourself they want you to stop it for them. I don't know what's so wonderful about men that you want to drop your income down to zilch in order to live with them, with no income at all. I don't know why they think they're so wonderful that you should want to do that for them.

'You can't live like that,' she persists. It seemed to me that life as a prostitute had to some extent destroyed her private life. 'Although you might take time off to be with someone, there comes a time when you've got to go back and find some clients to pay the bills, and so there's sulks and tantrums and rows and fights, and all the rest of it. But what is the alternative? Mostly they can't maintain you in the manner to which you've become accustomed. So really they're out of their class, but they're not prepared to say, "Right, I can see I'm out of my class here. I can't keep you in the manner to which you are accustomed, I'll have to go." They want to hang around being psychological wrecks.'

Helen had for a long time rented a number of properties so felt she always had the freedom to leave relationships and go elsewhere until she had calmed down. It meant she could be tolerant when perhaps she shouldn't have been. 'It meant I could be cool and block my mind off to him. He would try and be manly and storm out in a temper, thinking: Now she'll miss me, now she'll be sorry. And you were so relieved, really, as soon as you heard the car skidding down the driveway and out of sight. And you think: I hope he stays away for a few weeks. And then you think: Gosh, why should I have him back? I've had a wonderful few weeks without him. And that's where the crunch will come. You think: I haven't missed him, and he apparently wanted to leave me. And so you're quite surprised when some poor little dishevelled wreck ends up on your doorstep again, begging forgiveness. I can do without it.'

Although prostitution had given Helen a degree of financial independence as well as the strength not always to need a man in her private life, it turned out she had always rented, not bought properties. 'I didn't buy anything, but I certainly had access to money. If there were debts to be paid, I could always raise money. I was good at it. I was never good at lies – some women could winkle a couple of thousand out of a man in no time. I could never do that, but I could always winkle a hundred, and two or three of those a day when there was a crisis or some such ... Well, you could soon pay off any problems. But I never met men who were prepared to make sure that I didn't need to do that. They were already married, you see. And their wives weren't going to let go of a good deal like that. Because these were all good husbands – clients always tend to be good husbands – and there is no way that they are going to leave their marriages. So one is left with the dross.'

In her twenties, Helen remembers, with more than a hint of bitterness, she hadn't been able to meet any men she might have married. 'When you're virtually locked up by the Social Security, of course you don't meet anyone, you really don't. There you are, hidden away, and the only men you meet are the ones who come after you, the ones that want something out of you, saying things like "There she goes, the poor dear. I can spend a couple of nights with her, get some food, she'll prop me up a bit" – because women do, that's why we're so stupid.'

Helen worked as a prostitute for twelve years, only stopping recently when she had her second, late child. This time she found that the Social Security system had changed. 'It's much easier to lead a dignified life on Social Security now. And by this time, of course, I have the sort of things that you don't have with your first child – you don't have any furniture and you don't have any assets of any kind at all. In your forties you've got somewhere to live, you've got furniture, a cooker, gadgets, you've got this, you've got that. As unemployment increases, it's easier to stay on Social Security, and now that they pay the rent the money is workable. It's much easier to augment it a little bit, and nowadays you don't break the law by doing that. You can have a bit of extra money on the side, so without living in luxury, you can actually trog along okay. And now that so many people are there's no stigma left, you're not isolated any more, and really I'm living the way I think women ought to live.

'Women ought not to have grinding money worries when they're looking after small children. They should be able to take that time off. They should be part of society, out and about, going to playgroups for children, sharing interests with other women and leading a relaxed and happy life, not hidden or frightened or worried and taking it out on their children. Children can't grow up properly locked up and isolated.'

Her second child was a happy accident: 'I didn't realise I was pregnant until it was too late. It was one of those funny pregnancies. I'm glad it happened, very glad. Until then, between the first and the second, it had all been abortions. I thought: Jesus Christ, given what they put me through, never any more. But I'd look at the men and think that one big baby was enough without their little babies as well. If they'd go, I'd have the baby, but not both of them. Then I got into a situation where I could do that. He wasn't interested, so I could have the baby and not have him round my neck. That seemed to me a safe enough thing to do, but with the others I couldn't take on the man *and* the children, especially when they're very small. It's such a full-time thing, you need peace and quiet, all your energies and all your concentration. You don't want some neurotic man in the way.'

We sat and chatted animatedly, in the sunny room, about men and relationships. I too am a single parent, though I, unlike Helen, would have liked to be living with a man. Had she never found a man who was helpful? 'I've never met a man who was helpful, have you?' she responded. We both laughed, and agreed, in a light-hearted, conspiratorial way. But for me perhaps the laughter was more hollow than for her. She was in a profession where she continually brushed up against the more unpleasant side of men, and was completely disenchanted with them. I was not disenchanted with men in general. It was that specifically I would have liked more emotional support. Her view of men struck me as sad but inevitable, given her unfortunate experience of the Sixties. But Helen had chosen her path, and was not at all unhappy with it. Clearly, she has a full life with many friends. And she, like many women, married and unmarried, has chosen to find happiness through her children.

'Some women have husbands, and children,' she continues. 'If it's a good marriage they stay married to their husbands, but men like that have not come my way. I've seen them around, I've met them as clients – middle-aged men whose wives perhaps are not into sex with them any more because women's sex and men's sex doesn't necessarily coincide. Often they get bored with the same old routine, and because he's a gentleman he doesn't want to impose on her so he goes off elsewhere. He pays his money and takes his choice. And I would find that type of man much more desirable as a husband than the sort that I've had around me.'

For these men she does not necessarily have to be kinky – just a change. 'They want to be made to feel welcome. It wouldn't do for a prostitute to say, "Oh no, not that routine again." You've got to look as though you're enjoying it because otherwise they feel bad. You may enjoy it, it just depends. I mean, you may click. You probably won't but you may, and you've got to be sufficiently uninhibited to admit that, to enjoy it, to take what's on offer, accept it, be pleased with it – it's a nice bonus. But if you're not enjoying it you have to regard yourself as a professional – I'm getting the money, he's getting the understanding, so fair enough.

'There are some things that prostitutes don't like doing. Some of the very kinky things, like domination, sado-masochism, and humiliation take a certain personality, because otherwise you have to grit your teeth and that becomes stressful. But people like Lindi St Clair like it. They enjoy it, they love the drama of it, they like their work. As a prostitute you've got to be comfortable with what you take on, otherwise it becomes too stressful. If you keep on pushing yourself into situations which you dread or find repulsive then you do suffer psychological damage.'

Although Helen feels that it is possible to avoid this stress and wind up with your self-respect intact, it can affect all areas of the woman's life. 'Yes, it must do,' she confirms, 'for those who are not fortunate enough to be able to assert themselves in areas where they have enough choice, for women who feel that their job in life is to be walked over. Life must be incredibly stressful for them because they've got men at home walking over them, they've got the police walking over them, and they've got the roughest end of the clients walking over them. But for those women who weave their way around all that and decide what's okay for them, and make deliberate choices about what they do, I can't see that it does anyone any profound damage, quite honestly.'

She remained unmoved as she described the first time she had been with a client. This was a woman who had the strength to transcend her emotions. 'I felt dreadful. I thought: This is going to be dreadful, this man's old enough to be my father, this is going to be awful. But it wasn't. I found out that sex doesn't have to be with Adonis-like thirty-year-olds. It can be with all kinds of men – you never know which one's going to turn you on. Anyway, they don't have to turn you on. As long as you can feel the humanity in them, it's not necessary to be turned on. You can feel just as much job fulfilment in knowing that they appreciate what you're giving them.'

Another prostitute, twenty-four-year-old Suzie, who I met at a small late-night gathering at a friend's flat in Paddington, sees it differently: 'Sex is a very small part of the job. Most of the time is spent listening and chatting, keeping my mouth shut and saying only the right things. During the sex I think about what I have to do the next day, maybe make a shopping list. I don't get excited. I just switch myself off.' Her friend Tracey confirms this view: 'I cut off from the sex. If it takes more than thirty seconds I'm not doing my job. Two hours later I can't remember their faces.' Suzie did later admit that the first time she went with a client she cried a lot. 'It was horrible. It took me a long time to get used to it. But now there's nothing to it – most of them only want straightforward sexual intercourse and manual stimulation. You just lie there.'

Prostitute women are very vulnerable to attack, and it seems that most have some stories of physical violence to tell. One woman told me that once a man had threatened her with a knife and then beaten her up and stolen all the money she had earned. She was terrified. But despite this, the next day she was forced to go back out to work: 'I had bills to pay and my kid needed feeding.' She is constantly afraid when working.

Helen, on the other hand, has worked for long enough to develop a defensive tactic to deal summarily with potentially difficult or dangerous men. 'I wouldn't stand a rough, abusive man for two seconds, and they can tell it. They can pick that up in me instantly, that I'm not having it. They want me, and if they end up with me because they haven't quite understood what's on the other end of the telephone and they turn up at the door, I can repel them with a look. And then they won't come near me. That's come with experience, and with knowing that you've got a right to choose. You know that you're not going to be comfortable with this, and you've got a right to say no. You can say no and if they don't like it they're going to have to, as individuals, question themselves as to why someone won't have them even if they're paid to. And men in general are going to have to question themselves. But I'm sure men in general will behave themselves when they know women aren't going to put up with them!'

I had been told that Helen had started a union for prostitutes in 1975, called PLAN (Prostitution Laws Are Nonsense), but apparently I hadn't got it quite right. 'Oh, we never started a union, no. Prostitutes are loath to admit that they are prostitutes, never mind unions – that's all media hype. I ran campaigns for changing the law. But PLAN got swallowed up by the ECP [English Collective of Prostitutes, started in the late Seventies (see chapter 7)] and got squashed flat by the general feminist ethos of the Seventies and early Eighties. I got tired of banging my head against a brick wall. Also, the ECP hijacked the prostitution issue by making it into a kind of Marxist issue, and that got very tiresome.'

Helen spoke out indignantly against the English Collective of Prostitutes, based in seedy King's Cross, and their spokeswomen. But I felt that having some kind of organisation to represent and fight cases for prostitute women must be a good thing. Anyway, I was keen to hear her view as I hoped to interview Nina Lopez-Jones, one of the spokeswomen, though at that time she was proving unreasonably hard to pin down. (I spent a lot of time on the phone answering detailed questions about what it was exactly that I wanted to ask. Eventually I faxed them through a list of questions.)

Clearly, the representation issue was one that Helen felt passionate about. She talked accusingly of the activities and goals of the ECP. 'They don't want anything to change, they just want to carry on their divisive little ways. They don't represent people because they want to plant a dogma. Prostitutes drift into their sphere because of offers of help. They'll have a free legal aid afternoon – say, if you're caught soliciting you can come and speak to them. So women drift in through things like that, and then they find out that they've got to hate men. Although they're told, "We don't hate men, it's the feminists who hate men", you'll find that everybody at the ECP is a political lesbian – that in fact they find that most women aren't good enough to know, and certainly most men aren't. They want to break up any kind of meeting because the wrong kind of people might be present, so you can't get anything off the ground with them.

'They frighten the prostitutes away because they don't want to have to hate men, they frighten the media away by biting their heads off on the phone. They break up television programmes where the situation could possibly be aired for half an hour, but it's not aired because they're having fights with the producers. So I'm afraid that though their Marxist analysis has always been quite admirable, their strategies are just hopeless. They create the class divisions and gender divisions – they create it themselves and they nurture it themselves. They don't try to cross that divide.

'None of the inner circle at the ECP are prostitutes, they're all political lesbians. They're always looking for an enemy, and of course that's been the whole problem with Marxism – it's got to identify an enemy. And that is what has been so divisive and so oppressive. It's a great pity. There are all sorts of well-meaning people who'd like to know more, come to meetings, and not be seen off as blue-rinse Conservative ladies. A lot of blue-rinse Conservative ladies are very sympathetic, very sympathetic indeed. So are a lot of policemen, so are a lot of judges – why put these people off? I couldn't work with the ECP women, after the church sit-in [described in chapter 7], in which they seemed to delight in taking the bishop and people like that for a ride. It was too much for me, it was too nasty, and nothing was emerging, nothing had changed. There's not one single law that they have changed, there's no improvement that's been gained for the lot of prostitutes anywhere that they can lay claim to, not one. It seems to me that the proof of the pudding is in the eating. If in ten years they can't make some dent in the situation, have some friends in high places, bring some influence to bear, then they're not much use!'

Fortuitously, on my return home that evening I had a phone call from Nicky Adams, one of the spokeswomen from the ECP. They would, after all, agree to see me.

7

What I do for my husband is really no different

'You can't blame that on us,' responded the startled and faintly amused Nicky Adams who, together with Nina Lopez-Jones, I had come to meet at the King's Cross Women's Centre where the English Collective of Prostitutes is based. 'There are many things that haven't happened over the last ten years. The fact that more hasn't been done against prostitution under Thatcherism is a victory in itself!'

They were understandably not pleased that Helen Buckingham had been speaking out against the organisation for which they both act as spokeswomen. As a collective, they campaign for the abolition of the prostitution laws, so that the prostitute may have exactly the same rights as anybody else. They feel strongly that sex between consenting adults should not be the business of the law. They maintain that they have made a great deal of headway in this cause in terms of assisting prostitutes in fighting their personal cases, and generally standing up to police and other abuse.

To meet these women I went to a seemingly deserted address, a boarded-up shop front in a narrow side-street, and once I had been vetted via an intercom I passed through a heavy electronic door. Inside, the set-up was as lacking in frills but as full of earnest intention as any women's group meeting of my student days. The three small rooms were packed with people and every table and shelf was piled high with leaflets and files. Badges and T-shirts bearing legends such as 'Whores against Wars', 'Wages for Housework', and 'We Are All Bad Girls' were for sale at a nominal price to help support the cause. In the largest room a mother-and-toddler group for single mothers was meeting, in another a solicitor sat discussing a case. In fact, there was so much going on that, in order to talk, the three of us had to squeeze into the kitchen, which was barely big enough for our chairs plus an ever-busy kettle perched precariously on the draining-board.

The Collective was formed in 1975, and the petite Argentinian Nina Lopez-Jones with her pixie-cap of dark hair has been involved with it since 1978. 'It was formed,' she explained, 'to campaign for the abolition of all the prostitution laws. And also to campaign for better resources in the form of higher benefits, higher wages, student grants etc., so that no woman is forced to go on the game or to have sex with anyone because of poverty. We also campaign for any number of other resources – for example, housing, hostels, etc. – to help women who want to get off the game.'

The Collective works on a network basis: they're not a membership organisation, and there is no filling-in of cards with one's name and address. 'Prostitute women are illegal workers. Although of course the law says prostitution is not illegal really, you are an illegal worker because most women can't afford to come out. We felt that it was too dangerous to have the usual kind of membership, and that it wouldn't serve the purpose that we wanted, which is to really be accessible to prostitute women everywhere who want to be in touch with us about their working conditions, or anything that's happening in their lives that they feel the English Collective of Prostitutes can support them with. So we've been in touch with thousands of women over the years over any number of things. There are women who are either active in a long-term way within the Collective or who are active over a period of time while they are concerned about a particular issue in their lives – for example, fighting for custody of their children, or fighting an eviction because their landlord found out they were on the game, or fighting a case of illegality when they've been falsely arrested. We are as involved with women as they want to be involved with us.'

The Collective both campaigns for these women and runs legal and other services for them. On the one hand they want to change the situation for prostitutes, and on the other they deal with the day-to-day problems facing the women in the course of living their lives. 'That entails quite a lot of service work. For example, if you are working in King's Cross and you are living in a bed-and-breakfast hotel with two children, and you need housing in order to get off the game, we will, and we have, helped many women in situations like that to actually find accommodation from the council etc., and get off the game.

'But we have also been very successful at campaigning. We feel that people in general were once a lot more concerned with the morality of prostitution – for example, when I used to go out speaking ten years ago. They are not now. They know that it's immoral for women to be poor, and that if women refuse poverty by working as prostitutes they are entitled to do that. And that it should be every woman's right to do what she wants with her own body. She cannot be blamed for the situation of poverty that she is in and for wanting to get out of it. People really understand now that prostitution is about money, that it's not about whether you're into vice, or whether you're a nymphomaniac, or whether you've been raped as a child and therefore you cannot say no to sex any more. It's nothing to do with that – the basics of it is the money. I think that is a very big change. A lot of it has to do with our campaigning, but also with where people are coming from generally.'

One significant action taken by the women of the Collective was the occupation of their local church in King's Cross in 1982. In protest at what they saw as police illegality and racism in the King's Cross red-light area, they kept up the occupation for twelve days and drew a considerable amount of publicity. 'Many of the women who worked then were black, and the police were particularly picking on the black women, though they were also picking on the women who used our centre to get support for their cases,' explained Nina. 'The police used to park their cars outside the door and see who came in and out. When we had meetings we often had to call a solicitor or somebody to just escort women out from the Centre to the tube station so that they wouldn't get arrested on their way.

94

'The police were very upset that women were standing up to them, and were pleading not guilty, and asking for their right to a phone call when they were arrested at the police station, which at the time was unheard of. Many women suddenly started to plead not guilty when they were arrested. Women who worked in this area used to get arrested in the nearby little garden square. They used to go and sit on the benches there and have a cup of tea, and the police would come and drag them out and arrest them just because they were known to them.

'So instead of just putting up with this, many women, because they found out that we had started a legal service – and we used to go round leafleting, telling them that we are here and ready to help – they started to plead not guilty in court. And we organised for reliable solicitors to work with them, and the women won a number of the cases. The police were very upset. They started threatening women with losing custody of their children. They actually went to one woman's house, whose children were living with her mother, then told the grandmother that her daughter was on the game at King's Cross, which the grandmother did not know. And they threatened to take the child away and give the child to Social Services. There were any number of stories like that. It escalated to the point where we occupied the church because we felt that we had to make it public.'

The main result of the church occupation as far as the Collective were concerned was that public opinion did change: 'The church occupation was pivotal to that in the sense that it got a lot of publicity.' Another gain was to highlight a racist element in police behaviour towards prostitutes. 'At the beginning of the Eighties there was a lot of talk about police accountability generally, and what the police were doing in, for example, black communities. But nobody except us had connected that with what was happening to prostitute women, and the fact that if the police were being illegal in relation to black people – violent, beating them up etc. – they behaved to prostitute women in exactly the same way, if not worse, because as a prostitute you are considered to be a criminal.

'So if it was not acceptable that they behave in that way to black people, then it was also not acceptable that they do so to prostitute women. That connection was made and was very important, and a lot of people started to realise what the prostitution laws actually meant in practice, which they hadn't necessarily known anything about.

'There is a lot of ignorance around prostitution precisely because women are prevented from coming out and saying, "This is what's happening to me. This is what the prostitution laws mean in reality. These are all the civil rights I lose as a prostitute woman – the landlord can kick me out if he finds out, the Social Services can say I'm an unfit mother, and the taxi driver can charge me more." These are all the results of the legislation. It also means, for example, that you are cautioned by the police twice, and so before you even go to court, where you are judged on your record, you are labelled as a common prostitute. So the whole idea of being innocent until proven guilty as far as prostitutes are concerned is a complete lie. People don't know these things unless they themselves are prostitutes, so I think a lot came out [as a result of the church occupation] about policing and about prostitute women and how they are no different from anybody else.'

The boyish Lopez-Jones and the pretty blonde Nicky Adams wouldn't give much away about their personal background. The Collective have a policy of not saying who is a prostitute and who is not, and feel generally that it is imperative in the work that they do to remain relatively private. This, of course, is as intriguing as it is understandable. Nina has been with the Collective for many years more than Nicky Adams, in her twenties, who seems to be learning the ropes of spokeswoman from her older colleague.

'I wouldn't describe myself as somebody with a professional background,' Nina laughs mysteriously. She then goes on to shed some light: 'I am a campaigner. I came to England from Argentina in 1976, and I became involved in the Wages for Housework campaign [with which the ECP share an office], and through this I became involved with the English Collective of Prostitutes. I think that in order for you to understand the connection between the two organisations you have to realise that the Wages for Housework campaign focuses on women's poverty as well, and the fact that women's unwaged work is not recognised and therefore not paid, and that that's why when women get jobs outside the home we get a lot less money for them, because it's an extension of the work that we all do for free.

'We're against poverty generally and we don't see sex work as different from other kinds of service work that women have to provide, because women are always servicing men in one way or another. If you are somebody's wife you do many things for them, and in fact wives often come to the Collective and say, "Well, you know, I wouldn't necessarily say it publicly, but what I do for my husband is really no different. It's just I stick to the one man." I think that that's quite a widespread view among women. Wives are respectable, but they don't necessarily have a lot of protection.

'One of the things we have been involved in with Women Against Rape, which is another of our organisations based here, is precisely the campaign against rape in marriage, and to make the crime of rape in marriage illegal, which it was not. It was only made illegal last year [1991], so that by law until last year wives did not have the protection of the law. Two hundred and fifty years ago the judge who was involved in witch-hunts himself issued some statements, saying if you were a wife you really gave yourself to your husband for ever and you had no right to say no. Everybody took that as the law until last year, when it turned out that that wasn't the law at all. There was a case in which the [King's Cross Women's] Centre was involved in supporting the woman, and one of the things that the law commission who were looking into the issue of rape in marriage said was that wives had even less protection than prostitutes in relation to rape. That is true up to a point.

'In fact, prostitute women are in a very vulnerable position in the same way as wives were. If you are a prostitute and are raped, first of all you are not in a very good position to complain to the police about it because they might arrest you instead. Secondly, it's not taken seriously, and either the police or the court at any time can say, "She's a prostitute, therefore she can't be raped", or if she can be raped, "It's not that serious – it won't cause her any lasting damage because she is used to going with men anyway." There have been many cases like that, though this is also changing – there have been cases where judges have said that prostitute women should have the same protection as all other women. This is really a result of all the campaigning work that we have done, and also a result of women in general struggling and going to court. Every woman who is raped and goes to court is struggling for her life, saying, "Excuse me, I may be a prostitute, but he beat me up and raped me and I want justice." So we are part of a much wider movement.'

I was left still wondering what changes, if any, had actually been made to the prostitution laws since the Collective had begun their campaigning in 1975. Nina was gloomy: the changes that had been made were unwelcome. 'The changes have been bad, but it's been thirteen years of Tory rule and you don't expect many positive changes. What's happened is that the prostitution laws have been extended to men, to the clients. The kerb-crawling legislation was introduced in 1985, and it says that if you are a man who's soliciting for the purposes of prostitution and you solicit persistently – what they mean by that is that you have to approach two women or the same woman at least twice – you can be arrested for kerb-crawling.

'We campaigned against that in '84 and '85, and we formed a campaign against it which many other organisations took part in. The reason was that when the legislation was first presented they said it was for women's safety and women's protection and women's equality, and the way that they viewed equality was that since women were getting arrested then it was fair that the men should get arrested as well – while we were saying that since the men are not getting arrested the women should not get arrested either. Equality depends on which way you look at it – you can have equality up or equality down.

'But the Tories have definitely been into equality down. Women are losing their pensions now. Women used to get a pension at sixty, now they're thinking of changing it to only at sixty-five, because that's what men get. That has been the trend in relation to equality, and we made the case that we didn't want that kind of equality. We thought that sex between consenting adults shouldn't be the business of the law at all, and that there shouldn't be any prostitution laws – let alone extend them to include men.

'Also, it would give a lot of powers to the police. They would enforce it as a sus law, because the way the legislation is framed is like the three offences Act [a prostitute cautioned for soliciting three times will be charged] – that is, it relies on police evidence alone, they don't need any witnesses of any kind. They can just say, "Oh well, this guy was walking down the street and we saw him speak to two women." But the two women don't come to court to say yes, he approached me and was threatening or abusive or asked me for sex, or anything. There are no witnesses so the police can do what they like, because when it comes to the court case it's their word against the word of the person they accuse.

'The magistrates' courts are not known as fair courts. They are known as police courts, and even now, after all the evidence that has come out about police illegality and brutality in all kinds of places, and all the miscarriages of justice, you will find that magistrates are still reluctant to believe that the police can ever lie. In fact the police lie a lot, especially in magistrates' courts where they require very little evidence.

'Therefore, we said it was going to be a new sus law and that it was likely to be used particularly against black men, because it is our experience with the prostitution laws that the police often accuse black men of pimping. Not because black men are more likely to be pimps, but because it's just a way for them to get at black men who they want to get at for other reasons. We know many cases where, for example, the woman is white and has a black boyfriend, and they'll go after him and accuse him of pimping when he's just the woman's boyfriend and not a pimp at all. Also, from our experience of police racism in dealing with black prostitute women, we also knew that that was how they were going to implement the legislation against the men.

'We didn't actually win, in the sense that the legislation went through, but we won some changes. The House of Lords introduced an amendment saying that the soliciting had to be persistent or that it had to be likely to cause a nuisance, so that the police had to prove something, as opposed to nothing at all. And that has to some extent prevented an even greater abuse than what has already been happening. There has been plenty of abuse but it would have been much worse if that amendment had not been introduced, and it was as a result of our campaigning that it was introduced. There was another attempt, two years ago, to drop the amendment so that the police could arrest the men first time round, and we did manage to defeat that. It was Ken Livingstone who talked about it in the House of Commons, and he worked very closely with us, though we had quite a lot of support from any number of civil rights and civil liberties organisations, black groups, anti-rape groups and others.'

The Collective represent women from all walks of life, from the very young to grandmothers; some are ex-'sex workers', and some are still working; women of different races, immigrants, and women of English decent. The bottom line, Lopez-Jones makes it clear, is always money. 'It's either women who have been in a situation where they just don't see any other way out than to work as prostitutes. Or it's women who are not prepared to do the kind of jobs that women are prepared to do for the kind of money that those jobs pay, and who feel that they are better off as prostitutes. For example, if they are mothers, they can spend more time with their children, and they can afford to buy things for their children which they couldn't afford if they were on Income Support or if they were working in a factory or some other low-paid job.

'So it's a variety of reasons, because each one of us has particular reasons to do whatever we do with our lives. But at the same time there are many things that we have in common and money is one thing that all prostitute women have in common. And I think you'll find that money is something that normally all women have in common when you talk about their jobs. I don't know many secretaries who would be doing it for love if there was no wage attached to it.'

100

She feels that there are many women who prefer to work in an illegal profession because they can make more money. 'I think it's a question of what choices you have. As women, our choices are usually pretty bad, and we take the best out of the bad choices. I think that if most women had better choices they would not work as prostitutes, for many reasons. First of all it's illegal – a lot of it's illegal – it makes your life really difficult, and it means you have to lie to your family and you have to lie to your children most of the time. Some women do tell their families, but often you don't because it's too risky.'

This illicit behaviour is not, she believes, to do with morals. 'The point is that there is a lot of social stigma attached to the label "prostitution", and it's not necessarily that women are ashamed of it, because in fact I don't know anybody who is ashamed of it. Women pretty much feel that, look, I have a right to do what I have to do in order to survive, and I'm not the one to blame if my choices are not great. That's pretty much how women feel, but the stigma doesn't go away and the stigma would go away if there were no prostitution laws.'

The abolition of the prostitution laws would, she thinks, give women more choices. 'We're not into glamourising prostitution, and I know that some people who don't like what we say are into glamourising it as some kind of sex therapy, and a wonderful job, and really they don't know why more women are not doing it. I think it depends, quite frankly, on which end of the market you are working at. It's usually women who are making quite a lot of money at it and are not working on the street, who don't have to deal with a lot of police harassment, who glorify it in this way. We are not into glorifying, we don't think prostitution is great. One of our first slogans was that we are for prostitutes against prostitution. We don't think there should be any prostitution, but then there are many kinds of prostitution that women are involved in, and men also.

'There are many things that we have to do that we would rather not do. But in the world as it is at the moment all women must have the right to work as prostitutes if that's what they choose. There shouldn't be a set of laws that say if you work as a prostitute you're going to be persecuted and

101

prosecuted and we're going to make your life a misery. That should not happen.'

'We represent women who work in all kinds of places. Many women work in escort agencies or for Madams or do their own advertising. We're involved in all kinds of cases. The women in the Collective itself, who do the day-to-day work of keeping the Collective together, are both from the street and not from the street. But the women on the street have always been a point of reference for us as a Collective generally, in the sense that they are the women who know the most about the police, who are really at the receiving end of the prostitution laws. That is not to say that if you work from premises you are not at the receiving end of the police, because you are, but not in the same way.

'If you work from a flat you have to work alone, and if you work with somebody else it becomes a brothel, which is illegal, and the police can arrest you – which means that it is much less safe for women alone, because the men know that you are on your own and therefore are more likely to attack you. We've been involved in cases where women have been evicted because the landlord found out that they were working there, or women who were fighting for custody of their children because the school or social worker has found out they were working.

'There was one case where actually the police came to the woman's house in the middle of the day. In fact, two policemen had posed as clients to catch her – they just came and dragged the daughter out and gave her to Social Services. And then she had to fight to get her daughter back. The daughter hadn't up to that time known that her mother was on the game, so that the idea that this was bad for the daughter was ludicrous. It became bad for the daughter once the police got involved, because then she was separated from her mother. She was with Social Services, she didn't know what the hell was going on, and it was obviously a very traumatic experience. What was traumatic was not what her mother was doing, but what the police were doing to her and to her mother. After some months of battling it out, the daughter was allowed back with her mother. There have been many cases like that.

102

'A lot of the women working from premises complain about the police coming in and expecting free sex,' asserted Nicky Adams, leaning forward earnestly. 'Even if you may not be actually working illegally, working on your own, you're in a very weak position to insist that this doesn't happen, and to actually do something about it. Recently we had a whole spate of women coming to us for help with this, which was to do with a particular area where it was happening a lot. But even if they've managed to get assurances from the police that their complaint won't be used against them, they then run the risk of all kinds of things – like, for example, one woman has now had the planning department down on her in a way that wouldn't normally happen. They just wouldn't treat anybody else like that – the questions that they ask, the tone of voice, the general harassment. This is purely because they suspect that she is doing massage, you know, working on the game.'

'So,' continued Nina, 'the problem women working from premises have is that they have to work very hard to keep a good relationship with the police, to make sure they don't raid you. Often the police raid these premises following complaints from local residents, or you get right-wing councils deciding it's a good thing if they clamp down on prostitution – it looks good and therefore that's what they're going to do. A lot of it is to do with property value. The Tories, and right-wing people in general, are very good at telling you about morality. But what it comes down to is: "I moved into a red-light area and my house is worth this, but if it wasn't a red-light area my house would be worth twice as much, and therefore prostitute women should move out." We've seen that attitude in all the different cities that we've been involved with. In Southampton, for example, there was a whole issue of property values, and it has been the same in London.'

If you're working for an escort agency or a Madam, it seems that you don't get these problems with the police, and clearly you don't face the kind of harassment you would if you were standing on a street corner, visible and therefore accessible. But there are other problems. 'The fact that you are so completely underground really limits your possibilities in terms of what kind of recourse you can have if something happens

103

to you. In some ways the women who work on the street, precisely because most of them already have a record and have had so many arrests and all that, sometimes are able to be more open about what they do than women who work in an escort agency and lead complete double lives. Often nobody at all knows that the woman is on the game. The boyfriend doesn't know – he thinks that she's going out to some waitressing job in the evening, or whatever. It's really like that, so if something happens to you, what do you do? Who do you go to? Because it's going to come out.

'We've been involved with a woman who was raped, and she went to the police to tell them she had been raped, but she herself did not want to pursue it because, she said, "I can't afford the publicity. If people find out what I do I can lose a lot and I just can't afford it." But she wanted something to be done about this man because he's going around raping women, and she thought he should be stopped. So there she was in a complete catch-22 situation, because the police were putting pressure on her to take it through. They had had other complaints from prostitutes, but only with this woman did they feel they had a case.'

Most prostitutes according to the Collective have had some kind of violent experience, undergone some kind of threat, rape or assault, something that has been done to them against their will. And most of these women don't report it. 'The level of violence is high,' Nina confirms. 'It's so high that often if you ask women if there's a problem they say, "Oh no, things are fine", because they see violence as normal. Even when once there was a man going round trying to strangle women, it was a long time before it came out.'

One of the problems relating to violence for women working on the streets, according to the Collective, is that the police won't protect them. 'Women have reported assaults and rapes and even murders to the police, and the police won't do anything about it. We had a whole fight here with the police in King's Cross to get them to take violence seriously, and they won't. At some point they were looking out for a particularly violent man that they reported to us, and they said, "Can you tell all the girls?" We said, "Fine, we'll tell all the women we know, and put out the information, but what are you doing? After all, you're the ones who are paid to protect people."

'It turned out that they weren't doing anything. They were just waiting for some information to materialise, and in fact the people who were investigating the crime had not spoken to the Vice Squad. And the Vice Squad are the ones who actually arrest the women every night, and therefore can actually say to them, "This is what's happening, there is this violent man, and this is his description etc. Do you know anything?" No, there was no connection between the two.

'But if you speak to the police about what they are doing on kerb-crawling or on arresting women who are working as prostitutes on the street, they are very well co-ordinated. There are three police stations and the British Transport Police in King's Cross who cover the area very thoroughly, and every few months you see articles about how many women they have arrested, and how they are doing a great job keeping prostitution down successfully. But when it comes down to violence against women there is no co-ordination at all between police stations, not even between different units in the same police station. They put a lot more resources into prostitution than they do into violence, and that's why prostitution is dangerous. It doesn't have to be dangerous.'

According to the ECP's figures, approximately seventy per cent of all prostitutes are single mothers. One way they explain this relates to the high level of domestic violence in general. If you are going to be beaten up and/or raped anyway at home, it is not such a leap to risk it happening outside the home whilst at least earning a good independent living. Nina's evidence is alarming: 'Violence against women generally is very, very high. We worked with Women Against Rape, who did the first survey in 1985 of rape and sexual assault of women in London, and the figures that they came out with were absolutely staggering – one out of seven wives had been raped, in the home, where you're supposed to be safe.'

Again, the need for money is what it all boils down to: women will accept violence as a fact of life if it means they can be independent. After all, what makes women stay with violent men?' Nina asks rhetorically – 'The fact that they don't have an independent income. And that has been proved over and over again. Women who are being battered by their husbands or their boyfriends cannot leave because they don't have anywhere to go. Because they have children, they need a roof over their heads. They don't have an independent income so they stay, or even when they leave they are often forced to come back.

'It's exactly the same thing if you work as a prostitute woman. You need the money, and for many women if you have that independent income it means that you don't have to stay with that violent boyfriend. And I think that's often what people don't realise – they talk about the violence that's involved with prostitution but they don't think about the violence that's involved in the so-called normal relationships that are being promoted as this great family life. In fact, family life is one of violence, and many, many women precisely turn to prostitution as a way to have an independent income so that they can walk out of that kind of violence. It's a risk that's often worth taking, because if you know for certain that you are going to get beaten every time your husband gets drunk you're better off standing on a street corner.'

Nina has some rather depressing statistics, she claims, which show that the great majority of women have been raped or sexually assaulted in some way. But surely, this did not necessarily mean it would be an easy matter to face violence on the streets?

'Having the money,' she pointed out, 'is also a way of avoiding a lot of other rape and violence in your life generally, whether from your family or not. It means that you can afford to take a cab rather than waiting out on the street for a bus and running the risk of being attacked there. It means that you don't have to work necessarily in a job where either sex with your boss, or some kind of sexual work with your boss, is a requirement. It means you don't have to sleep with your landlord so that he doesn't evict you.'

According to the women of the ECP, prostitution is in many ways more honest than some other money-based relationships.

'Because money comes into everything – it shouldn't but it does, because that's the kind of society we live in. Money determines how you are treated, it determines where you live, it determines what kind of police protection you get, it determines what school, what education – everything is determined by what your income is and your background, whether you've had money for generations or whether this is the first generation. Money determines all our relationships and it determines that men are violent to women because they have a lot more money and a lot more power than women do.

'But relationships in general are not seen like that. They are seen as psychological, nothing to do with economics. But when it comes to prostitution nobody can avoid the fact that there is an economic transaction going on and that the woman is definitely doing it for the money – that's what she gets for it. It's the same all over. It's just that when it comes to prostitution, it's clear, the cards are on the table. With everybody else the cards are under the table. And that's why many men like going to prostitutes, because there's no involvement, you know exactly what the transaction is, you don't have to pretend to be in love, you don't have to pretend to be interested, you don't have to pretend all these things. It's in that sense a cleaner relationship.'

Most of the women I'd met hadn't become rich through prostitution, they all spent the money as quickly as they earned it, though everyone did seem to know of someone who had managed to save and put a deposit down on their own home. But for the most part the tragedy lies in the quickly earned and quickly spent nature of the money gained from selling sex. The money you actually get varies.

'It depends where you work. You can make thirty pounds or twenty pounds a trick, so it depends how many tricks you get a night. Or you can work in some other place where you make a hundred and fifty pounds a trick, but then it takes three hours rather than ten minutes, and you have to go out for dinner. Or you can get five hundred pounds for the night, or you can get two hundred pounds for the night, or you can get three thousand pounds for a weekend. It depends at what level you work. At some levels the money is relatively big and at others it isn't.'

For Nina and the Collective, the notion of prostitution is much broader and certainly less sharply defined than twenty or thirty pounds for ten minutes of sexual intercourse. 'Some women manage to make it in some other way. There are many ex-prostitutes who then become famous actresses or singers or marry a rich guy etc., and gain respectability in that way, having started off as prostitutes. You don't necessarily know, and they don't necessarily advertise it, but everybody knows that, for example, in the film industry unless you prostitute yourself you don't get there. The amount of sex work that women have to do is enormous. That's one of the issues we take up with the Wages for Housework campaign, where we are campaigning to get all women's work recognised and counted in the GNP of every country, so that all the work that women do is recognised. Motherhood, looking after everyone, servicing everyone, agricultural work that women do for free – there's an enormous amount of work that women do for free all over the world. Sex work is part of that work, and we of the English Collective of Prostitutes want sex work to be counted in it.'

When I asked Nina and Nicky what they felt ought to be particularly emphasised about their campaign, Nina responded with righteous indignation: 'Prostitution is always looked at as this really separate thing – "There are these women who do this separate thing that nobody else does." As it turns out, most women are involved in sex in one way or another, so the idea that there is something specific about prostitution is absurd. Promiscuity is now quite widespread, so the gap is really not very big. The difference is that if you do it in one way it's legal and if you do it another way it's not, and therefore you have the police and all sorts of other people after you.'

In the end, we came back to the issue we had started with: what they are saying is that the prostitution laws ought to be abolished. Nina is emphatic: 'The prostitution laws are there to tell all women that you have to be respectable and poor and not have too many expectations when it comes to money.

108

Prostitute women have much higher expectations when it comes to money, much higher expectations that all women should have. In breaking down the divisions between prostitute women and other women we raise every woman's expectations, and that is very dangerous for the establishment. But it's not an easy task, so that's why the prostitution laws are still there. There's a lot more at stake in abolishing the prostitution laws than whether or not a few thousand women get arrested every year. What's at stake is what all women are going to want for themselves.'

8

People want to be ripped off

'People who normally would not dare to express their fantasies find acceptance here,' explains Tuppy Owens, well know publisher of the *Sex Maniac's Diary* and other erotica and unrepentant swinger, of her recent Sex Maniac's Ball, a charity event for which guests were paying up to £80 as ticket for an evening of debauchery which promised adult baby play, a Black Mass in the dungeon, a Miss Prim of the Muir Reform Academy in attendance complete with cane, an Auction of erotica, a Geisha display, Dane's rubber accessories and a sponsored striptease, among other entertainments. The Ball has been held annually since 1986.

'People dressed mainly in leather,' a boyfriend, an inveterate party-goer, described the Ball – 'black and sinister, or wittily revealing! I spoke to a small, dark man, dressed in black,' he continued, delighted to be of assistance in my research, 'who led a pretty blonde topless girl around on a chain that was threaded through loops attached to her nipples. The man explained, "We were getting a bit bored of straight love-making and this heightens the intensity of the relationship between us. I think it's important to explore your feelings together." I saw transvestites and cross-dressers milling about in "kinky corner". And small groups of people were entering a large "fondling box" which was peppered with arm-sized holes for external access. I watched them re-emerging some minutes later breathless, dishevelled and amused.'

Tuppy, organiser of the merry debauchery, greeted me amicably one morning, breathless from wending her way through the dark passages and stairwell at the entrance to her basement flat, both office and home, in a smart Mayfair block. In the dim light of her exotic surroundings she could have passed for a leggy teenager, in her black shorts and sneakers, her casually

110

loose pony-tail bouncing about. But apparently a teenager in the Fifties, she must be nearly fifty by now. She runs the Ball in order to raise money for her charity, the Outsiders Club. This trust, with its regular meetings, is there to help disabled people express their sexuality, for, as Tuppy once put it, 'If a man has no arms, he can't even masturbate.'

She is undoubtedly a Sixties person, a product of her generation. She discovered sex in the Sixties, had a wonderful time and has never let go. She is generous-spirited and generous-minded. She talked freely with me over large cups of coffee, in her dusky-pink flat with its flatteringly low lighting.

She grew up in a large house in rural Cambridgeshire, the only girl among several older brothers. Tomboyish and sexy at the same time, she was dubbed Tuppy because she was 'only a tuppenny-ha'penny girl'. Then she went to Kenya, 'then to the Serengeti, because I was interested in ecology. So I went on to Exeter University. Then I came to London and worked for the Natural Environment Research Council, which was a government job, and I just didn't really like working for the government – a bit too humdrum.

'At the time I had a boyfriend whose father was a printer, and I saw the sex books that he was printing. They were ridiculously bad and I thought I could do some myself. So I produced a book called *Sexual Harmony*, just at the same time as the sex supermarkets were starting, and the book sold amazingly well. People were actually laughing and smiling and looking passionate instead of shifty. And then I thought I'd set up and do more. I didn't get any money for the first one – I'd just done it to show how it should be done properly. So I thought I'd set up a publishing company. I did my own books, that were also sexual books, but they were a bit more adventurous. I did a series called *Love in the Open Air*, so I did *Spring*, *Summer*, *Autumn* and *Winter*, with one man and two women photographed in the open air. And then I had the idea for the *Sex Maniac's Diary*. That was a sort of instant hit, and obviously more profitable than the picture books.

'The *Diary*'s now been going for ages and ages. To begin with it looked very straight, apart from the fact that it had different sexual positions for every day of the year beside the

111

date. I made it look very straight so that it would look something like a gardener's diary or some such at first glance, but it had things about sex parties and erotic hotels listed. First of all, I didn't know much about erotic hotels and clubs and things like that, but then I built up the research for the different sections – though most people wouldn't buy it for things like that, they just buy it as a laugh and don't take much notice. But politically sex has now become much more interesting. It's become a political issue, and in fact anyone in the business would say it's become quite boring at the moment because you spend half the time defending what you do.'

Tuppy didn't seem particularly worried about how people outside the professional sex world reacted to the work she does. She considered: 'I suppose they think I'm slightly adventurous. It depends who you mean by "people", really. There are lots of different people out there who would have lots of different opinions about me – they're probably mistrusting.'

While sex is often seen as a sleazy industry, a man's world, and a woman in any area of it is often, like a prostitute, devalued, Tuppy has quite a different view. 'I look upon it as part of my role to take it out of the sleaze, although I'm not totally against sleaze, really. I think there's room for everything – even the very basic porno that used to be produced, the seedy stuff. Not *Mayfair* or *Penthouse* or *Playboy* stuff. It was, you know, some girl paid seven pounds to take her knickers off in a back room, and the pictures were produced by somebody that wasn't particularly artistic, and printed quickly. They were called five-bob arts and people loved them. In a way, that was part of the fun of the Fifties, I guess. I think that's as relevant to it all as the glamorising, expensively produced magazines are now. In fact, I think the glamorising actually detracts from the passion, the instantaneous lust of it.'

Tuppy doesn't feel that the women are exploited. 'They might not like the person they work for, but most people hate their bosses – you probably don't like your publisher that much – it's quite normal. But I've never known anybody who feels exploited – even, for example, the girl who's paid seven pounds to take her knickers down. A lot of people would think:

Brilliant, you go in and take your knickers down, you get your money. In those days, the Fifties, that would be quite a lot of money. You could go out and have a good night out on it and that was easy money. I really love the idea that I produce twenty thousand erotic books and they're going to go out and produce twenty thousand orgasms, and people are going to be jerking off over what I produce and have pleasure out of it. That's great, I think that's normal.'

There is a lot of research involved in the preparation of the *Diary*. Tuppy subscribes to a multitude of international sex magazines, and also gets people to gather them up for her from their travels round the world. 'A lot of time is spent reading the magazines, and then from that reading matter I collect quotes for the *Diary* which are funny things people have said or other things to do with sex. I find out what's the scene this year. I always think: I've done all this now, I won't have to change it much for next year. But by the time next year comes things are quite different – obvious things, like more sleazy clubs have closed down or changed their names or things like that. Also, I suppose because sex is such a spontaneous thing, the passion for a club that's really good can collapse within the year. But just as stuff is getting old and dying out there's always new places opening, and people like Annie Sprinkle [a sexual performer] having shows and being written about in the national press.

'Now there are things like the meeting yesterday at the Gay and Lesbian Centre. There are three lesbians who produced a lot of lesbian sexual material, and then were very insulted because some of the lesbian and gay bookshops wouldn't stock it. And they called a meeting. Well, if people don't stock my books I just think: Oh shit, I'll just go somewhere else. After all, you've got to sell your books. Well, because those are the only bookshops serving the community these three think that the lesbians going into the shops should be allowed to see erotic images, and so they called a huge meeting – incredible! There's that sex-positiveness coming out of that group, and it's really quite exciting. I saw it coming from feminism, women being more interested in sex and more willing to say so, and really being offended by people thinking that they're not. It's

113

not a change for women at all, just that women haven't dared to say it before. Most women love sex.'

With much of the sex-industry output being aimed at men, it was interesting to hear Tuppy's view that many women buy sex magazines. 'Often they like buying them to excite their husbands,' she elaborated, 'but they're not ashamed of buying them. What tends to happen is that after childbirth the sexual urge is diverted into love for children, and usually after child-birth women go off sex for a bit, and then it comes back. But I'd say that on the whole they love sex as much as men. It's quite interesting about group sex and orgy parties and things like that. Mostly in a marriage the man drags the woman along and she thinks: Oh, this is boring – I really just want my husband doing it. And then half-way through the night she suddenly gets turned on and she's still fucking and he's saying, "Come on, now, we've got to go home" and getting really jealous.

'And everybody knows that always happens at swing parties. Women might be more reluctant to begin with because they've been brought up to think it's wrong, or maybe never thought about it. I think that men, having an external organ that they're aware of, are much more aware of their sexuality. Women often don't learn to masturbate until they're older, and often don't think about their sexuality because they're told not to. Otherwise, I don't think there's much difference be-tween men and women. Women have even become quite aggressive now – they go out in gangs and try to pull men. They've always been able to do this and always have done it, individually.'

Her *Diary*, she makes clear, is aimed at men and women equally. 'The only trouble is that there aren't a lot of strip clubs for women. There just aren't the same facilities for women, brothels for women and that, so most of the places are male-orientated. But that's not my fault – its just what's there. As far as I'm concerned, I write the *Diary* for myself really, so if I was going to Barcelona what would I want to do? I'd want to see a sex show and go to clubs, so I find out those things. I think about what my male friends would want, and often it's all come anyway from my friends' trips. I should think I know about a hundred people around the world who travel, and first of all ring me up, because I might know much more than was in the last *Diary*, and then they do the trip and then they write it up and tell me about it. It's actually quite exciting for them because they've got a double reason for going to see these places.

'Last year I actually reduced the *Diary* down to a pretty minimal level, for business reasons, and produced a separate *Sex Maniac's Bible*, which is a much bigger book and covers everything. The *Diary* mainly has listings, but this is more of a travel book and a guide to what's happening in the world of performance art, libraries which have collections of erotica, and how to get to them – things like that – so it's much more comprehensive.' Tuppy gave me a copy of the *Sex Maniac's Bible*. It is full of nude photos and cartoons, sections on shopping, playing, clubbing and travelling. There is a delightful article on belly-dancing, and a section headed 'Talking', which contains useful phrases for the traveller in twelve different languages – such as 'I can't understand a word you're saying: let's just make love' in Spanish or Japanese, 'I can't take any more!' in Hebrew or French, or even 'My wife and I would like to make it with you', in Swedish or Russian.

Now Tuppy is slowly building the *Diary* back up again, to be more fun than it was last time. 'But,' she says, 'I wanted people to buy the *Bible* as well last year – it's hard to survive on something that just sells annually. The *Diary* now sells at sex shops, newsagents and gift shops. W. H. Smith sell it in their airport shops, Vivienne Westwood sells it in her shop – some people just like it.'

All this has had some effect on her private life. 'In all the long-term relationships I've had the guys have got pissed off with all the sex, sex, sex all the time. One guy I was going out with didn't like my job at all. I used to drag him off to sex parties and he used to cry – well, almost, but not quite! I don't go to sex parties any more. But the women who do go are just ordinary women. I wouldn't go to a sex party again unless I was in a relationship that really went down that avenue, going off and having group activities. I wouldn't do it out of choice for myself, but I might do it as an erotic adjunct to something else. Mostly I went, I think, because I was just so pleased to find – in my fantasy, when I was about twenty-one, I used to see myself running a sex club – that there really were sex clubs. I just had to go. And my boyfriend at the time never found out about the sex parties (he was the one with the father who was the printer who did the sex books) – he was horrified to find out that I was interested. He just thought: Oh come on, Tuppy, you can't mix with people like that.

'So I met all these swingers in London who were quite middle-class, professional people and they were part of the swing routine. It was raunchy in that they were not just a lot of horny guys, but they'd drag in as many willing, sexy women off the streets as they could, and fuck them as much as possible. But nevertheless a lot of women with them were highly sexed women – they weren't pushing women into it, just trying to find as many horny women as they could. It was a bit cold, definitely cold. I just used to think that was the worst sex you could have – a guy would just get on top of you and come. I even had an experience when I said, "I'm not on the Pill, please don't come inside me." And then the guy did, and they all laughed and said "It's all right, he's an abortionist, ha ha, ha ha." The bastards.'

Later in the Sixties a younger, more experimental crowd came along, a new group of people. 'But I got a bit annoyed with it and I thought I didn't want to be part of a crowd, I just wanted to be on my own. I still go to S and M clubs, where everyone gets dressed up. They're sort of night-clubs, and they're very erotic. There's no sex, just people being erotic – it's fun to dress up. But I don't go much any more because I'm too well known. I used to be able to hide behind the *Diary*, but now that I run the Sex Maniac's Ball every year everyone knows who I am.'

Tuppy had the idea for starting the Sex Maniac's Ball when she was travelling in America. 'On a research trip I was staying with a lot of the people listed in the *Diary*, and I got about three quarters of the way round, and I thought: This is ridiculous, all the people I've visited would love to meet each

116

other, but they will never meet because there's no place for them to meet. And I thought I should hold an event where all the people who are interested in the *Diary* could get together, and I could do it in London first and then in America. Then I thought it would be great because I could do it as a fund-raising event, because I run an organisation to help people with social disabilities have sex.

'That was an amazingly lucky decision, because the Ball works mostly because of the fund-raising aspect of it. It doesn't raise that much money but it does raise a bit. We have things like people with foot fetishes going round and kissing people's feet, which is quite amusing. Normally, if a foot fetishist comes up to kiss your feet you might not be keen, but if it's for charity you just let him do it. So people move on a bit. And since it's everything that's in the *Diary* you get the swingers, and the adult babies and the curious, and the people with individual fetishes – everybody comes, and some of the physically disabled people as well who the charity is for. So everybody is learning really to accept things they might see as being very weird. I've only ever done it in England, never in America, and I don't think I could do it anywhere else now as it takes months of preparation. But it's all quite outrageous, really! Although in England we've got no pornography (as compared to the extremes of foreign pornography) and no hard-core sex shows and that, when foreigners come here they think we're really wild. It's strange – actually, the average American is quite prudish.'

Tuppy once took advantage of an opportunity to act in a pornographic film. She didn't appear to think she was much good as an actress, but she did say that once she relaxed into it she enjoyed herself. She was in fact so relaxed that when at one point in mid sex scene she felt like peeing, she simply let herself go and did so on camera. She found it liberating and fun, but probably wouldn't repeat the experience.

Wallowing in the fun of the sex world as she does is one thing, but Tuppy is realistic about many people's attitudes. 'There are a lot of people who are, I suppose, only in porn for the money, who pay as little as possible for as much as possible.

117

And that is probably what most people, the public, see, because that's what's successful. And there's this awful suspicion I have that actually people want to be ripped off, they don't want to really know what's going on in their sex lives – they want to have dreams, they don't want them to be smashed. As long as they have that fear of pleasure there is room for exploitation. Otherwise, how could those sex shops filled with ridiculous and over-priced and non-working things survive?

'It's something I haven't really got to the bottom of, I think. You can go into a sex shop and say, "What is the problem that most people come into the shop with?" – after all, most go in there because they're not happy sexually – and they'll say, "Premature ejaculation". And the thing that gets sold to these people is a thing called Stud, which actually numbs the top of the prick. Well, as a trained sex therapist, I know that the worst thing you can ever do to a person with premature ejaculation is to numb their prick. The cure is to actually become more aware of the penis and not less. So, basically, the sex shops have been selling something for years that makes people worse off than they were already. And they say there just wouldn't be a market for anything that's really helpful. People don't really want the truth – it's weird, isn't it?'

Easy-going but earnest, Tuppy's overriding aim is to further her charity work for the disabled and to help people in general sexually. 'A lot of people are helped through the *Diary* – not only socially, but they get less worried about themselves because they read that there are organisations that cater for their tastes, and they become more tolerant towards people with other tastes. London's most well known top dominatrix has met her man through the *Diary*. She's a woman called Claire. She's probably not as well known as Lindi St Clair, actually, but Lindi's more well known now because she's been running the Corrective Party. She's asked me to stand as a candidate, but oh Gawd...' Perhaps even for Tuppy, enough is enough.

9

It makes her feel very feminine and very powerful

The tall, smartly dressed figure of Isabel Kaprowski, a self-confessed 'hardened, jaded pornographer', came smilingly to meet me one chilly autumn morning in a suitably bohemian Covent Garden café. In her early thirties, she is managing editor of the soft porn magazines in the Portland Publishing group like *Penthouse* and *Forum*. And, unlike Linzi Drew, she was not put into the job for the purposes of public relations: she is actually the editor. We ordered coffee and croissants and soon discovered that we knew people and places in common. We'd both studied at University College London, she having obtained a degree in Classics and I in Anthropology, and she knew a colleague of mine at *Woman's Journal*, both having attended North London Collegiate. And that's probably where the similarities ended. Hers did, after all, seem an unusual career to follow – for someone who gave every appearance of being a bluestocking.

'I don't think it's odd at all,' she countered. 'A lot of classical literature is very sexy, some of the myths, and poetry, like Catullus. I loved all that when I was at school and at university, and if I ever do a PhD, as I'd like to, perhaps when I'm sixty, it'll be about erotic poetry. So really, it's just one of my main interests.'

She pondered the question of her own sexuality. 'I think my mother did the best job she could. She believed she was extremely sexually liberated – I actually don't think she was nearly as sexually liberated as she thought she was, and she possibly would even recognise that herself now. Compared to mothers of other people, she was not bad. She dressed attractively, she could still get whistles in the street in her forties – and possibly later, I don't know. And without really knowing about it, as a child I sort of did pick up that women have a sexuality as well – it wasn't just something that men did to women. I was also brought up as a Catholic, which was very confusing because it made me feel . . . it was all a bit complicated.'

Isabel was significantly affected by a negative sexual experience in her childhood. 'I was sexually assaulted when I was nine – not by someone in my family, thank God, but by someone I knew quite well, someone I was very fond of. I had a real crush on him. He was eighteen years old and he took advantage of me. What was most damaging about it wasn't just the physical side, but the emotional side, because I thought that after what happened, even though I didn't enjoy it, there was a sort of relationship there, and there wasn't.

'The portcullis came down the next day. It was just like his old ways, he was teasing me. I was just a little girl, that sort of thing. I didn't realise I'd been sexually assaulted – and, of course, he swore me to secrecy – until I was thirteen and my mother got this book out of the library about disturbed children, which included asthmatic children, because I'm asthmatic, and the book had a section on sexually abused children. And being very interested in anything to do with sex, regardless of what it's about, I immediately read that, and I suddenly realised that I had been sexually assaulted. And I told her. I hadn't said anything to anybody for four years, and it made me feel awful. I'd been interested in boys up to then, and then I just decided that no, they were animals, and I went back into the Catholic Church.

'When I finally did lose my virginity properly, it was a big decision to make. Not only did I have to face my Catholic guilt, but also I knew I had a very tough hymen, and the memory of sexual assault. I had to cope with all that. And when I did make love for the first time, it was absolutely the most phenomenal thing. It was very, very painful to start with. It took him about three hours altogether. He was very experienced. He didn't give up, he just kept coming off me and doing something else, then starting again. How he managed to keep it up, literally, I do not know! I was very, very lucky in my first lover. But he did keep it up, and when he did finally get inside me I felt amazing and I just thought he had put something in my drink. I thought I was on drugs, I was absolutely out, it was wonderful.

'So after that I became extremely keen on sex, and if the Catholic Church says that sex before marriage is wrong – how could sex be wrong? It's absolutely wonderful. So I pulled away. Plus, I got close to my grandmother on the Jewish side of the family, and as I got older I became more Jewish. Particularly since I met Jonathon, my husband, who is Jewish, I've gone for that side.'

Having now spent most of her life happily concentrating on sex and editing pornographic magazines, she has fond memories of her induction into the business, which happened by chance when she met Tuppy Owens through a mutual friend at the flats where she was living in 1982. 'I was at London University, and Tuppy said she needed some help with the *Sex Maniac's Diary* at Easter time, so I gave her my phone number. I just thought she was such an outrageous person, and so interesting. I'd always been very interested in sexual things and I thought it would be fun to do, and I could do it in the holidays. Anyway, much to my amazement she actually did ring up three months later and say, "Would you like to do some proof-reading?" So I did, and I just killed myself over it. I had seen the *Diary* before in shops but had only flipped through it and never actually bought it. I really enjoyed it.

'So I did that for two or three years and then in October 1985 the editorship of *Forum* became vacant and Tuppy rang me up and said, "You've got to go for this job." And I said, "I can't possibly go for the job", because, you know, the editor of *Forum* is like this great guru-type person up there, and while I was very interested in sex, I didn't regard myself as a guru – besides which, I had paid my part-time PhD fees to do my doctorate. So she said, "I'm not doing this for you, I'm doing it for the magazine. The magazine's got really dire, and you're the only person I know in the whole world who can do it!" So I thought: Well, I'll meet the guy for lunch – there is such a thing as a free lunch. And I met the guy for lunch and that was virtually it. Everybody who starts in the editorial department there is on three months' probation, so I thought: Well, they'll just chuck me out after three months. But I was wrong. I was quite honest about my lack of editorial experience; and they were very happy with me. I just didn't do my PhD.'

Isabel's parents were amazed when she told them about her work, and she remembers her mother, particularly, being rather pleased about it, commenting at the time, 'You seem to be tailor-made for that sort of job!' Her father was more ambivalent, but, she says, 'when I was on *Penthouse* my father was more pleased about that, as he used to read the magazine.'

There had never been a female editor at *Forum* before. Though women like Anne Hooper and Anna Raeburn had written for the magazine, this was quite a dramatic change. But as a woman Isabel didn't find herself compromised by the position she'd taken on. On the contrary: 'I'd been interested in erotic literature from an early age, and really what it did was give me an excuse to talk about sex all the time.

'And nobody could tell me off any more. When people said, "Oh, you always want to read dirty books", or "You always want to see the sexual innuendo in something", for a change I could say, "That's my job." So it was wonderful. But I always thought of *Forum* as not being just an erotic magazine – it had an authority about it. It had medical things and psychiatric things as well as the more obvious turning-on sorts of things. I thought it was very respectable – not that I think that something that is purely devoted to erotic entertainment is something to be looked down on, either.'

Isabel's friends generally thought the job was a great laugh; or, like her mother, they thought it was the perfect job for her. She experienced no disapproval, perhaps because her friends had grown accustomed to her fascination with sex over quite some time. 'I remember,' she grinned infectiously, 'when I first started secondary school I went round on the first day telling everyone the facts of life that I'd just been told by my mother. And I suppose I got a bit of a name for myself. But I didn't mind at all, it was great fun. I think I've been sexy from an early age, and I think in fact an awful lot of children are, but often what happens is that their parents make them feel ashamed about it, and they end up not enjoying it later on, particularly women, because they're made to feel that nice girls don't.'

Working for *Forum* liberated Isabel completely, removing even the smallest remaining inhibitions (such as a slight prejudice that she'd had towards gay people), although her social life has calmed down a lot since her marriage two years ago, because she wanted a monogamous relationship. In the early stages of her new job she was able to go out and open herself up completely to learning about and experiencing the diversity of the sex scene. 'I used to go to fetish clubs and meet male transvestites in their rubber dresses – it was all very interesting. I'm not really into the S and M scene but I did go and see. When I first started on *Forum* a very experienced *Forum* writer said, "I must take you to a fetish and S and M club", and he'd warned me that it might be a little bit heavy. There was a man who got whipped by a woman, but he wasn't tied down. There I was watching with interest and he suddenly went very green about the gills and said, "I've got to go home", which was quite funny.

'It was really lovely when I went to lots of other clubs as well, because people who like dressing up in rubber, or whipping each other or spanking each other, they know that they've got a minority interest. If they can go to a club and feel safe then they can really come out and be very frank about it. What I liked about it was that instead of pussy-footing around pretending that you were just meeting socially, people know that actually you want to get to know someone sexually.

'I also once went to a swing party, which was a bit of a disaster. It was in London. I'm not terribly into swinging because it's too prearranged. If I was still single I'd want to have my sex spontaneously – I might want to have two or three lovers at one time but I certainly wouldn't want to feel that it had been organised. But a man I knew had been pestering me for about a year to go to a swing party and I'd run out of excuses. Originally I'd said that my leg, which was hurt in a car accident, would sort of seize up and then the ambulance would have to come and the police would come . . . but I ran out of excuses so I went.

123

'We had to turn up at eight o'clock because you have to have a quorum for these things. I was going to a gay book launch earlier, so I went to that and turned up at half past ten. I'd been told there was going to be a "knitting room" for people who didn't absolutely want to have to join in. I thought that by the time I rolled up at half past ten there'd be a seething mass of writhing bodies and, you know, that I'd probably join them, get caught up in the excitement of it. I walked into the "knitting room", and all these people were sitting around very rigidly, arms crossed, and nobody really chatting anybody up – really, really odd. And my arrival seemed to act as a catalyst, not because I was so attractive but because I was the first new person to have arrived, and somehow it got things going.

'But I didn't want to have to sleep with any of the men, I didn't fancy any of them. I suppose if I had fancied any of them I might have, but I didn't. Couples would go off hand in hand to rooms equipped with plenty of condoms, and when they came back they looked very proud of themselves, but there was this feeling from the men that, well, you really ought to be doing this. And I didn't like that, I really didn't, so I never want to go to a swing party again. It isn't my sort of thing. I'd rather have my sex privately or have it publicly but spontaneously.'

She has the same theory about swinging as Tuppy Owens. If it is your sort of thing, she says, it is usually, initially, something that the man wants to do; he wants to get his woman to go along because really he wants to have it away with someone else. 'So he'll spend a long time trying to persuade her to go, and eventually she'll say yes, she'll go to the party. And then the woman finds that she's able to have sex with lots of people and really have a wonderful time, and the man often ends up getting very annoyed about it and dragging her off home. I think that's interesting – people think it's all for men, when actually it's the women. I also think that it's silly that at some parties there's a requirement that there should be no single men, because you need more single men to go round! Well, you do in a way, if a woman's going to be properly satisfied.'

Isabel has managed to have a great deal of fun as editor of *Forum*, and at the same time learnt a lot about other people's sexuality – 'gay or straight or bisexual, though in fact a lot of people don't want to be labelled in any particular way. And I've always enjoyed hearing about other people's sexual escapades anyway, whether it's been readers or contributors, or people you meet at parties. Most people are interested in *Forum*. If you meet them socially they want to know are the letters genuine, and then they'll talk about a friend they've got who might say this, that or the other.

'But obviously, you try to treat people with respect. I think that particularly with the backlash of Aids there's an awful lot of emphasis in the press and other media for everybody to be heterosexual, everybody to be married and have two point three children, and it's just ridiculous. It's not possible for many people. Many people want to have other ways of living, so I think that *Forum* is very important in making everybody feel that, apart from if you're a paedophile or a rapist, whatever you do sexually is acceptable. Also I learned about fetishes I didn't know existed, like people who find fur sexually attractive, or people who like dressing up in nappies pretending to be babies, which is nothing to do with paedophilia at all – it's that they want to be treated like babies.'

She remembers once meeting a rather attractive transvestite in a fetish club. 'He wore a bright-red rubber dress, which was quite fun. He was very keen to meet for a date, so I thought that would be okay. Anyway, it became very clear during the course of the evening that he was far more interested in getting into my wardrobe than getting into my knickers. Not that I was particularly eager to go to bed with him right away anyway, but I actually didn't really fancy the idea of him coming home and trying all my clothes on. Maybe I didn't like him very much. I remember trying to get away from him, and he insisted on getting the bus with me to go home, and tried to get into my flat, and that was pretty horrible. So I just had to be very firm and tell him to go, nicely, but firmly. It was all a bit of a shock.

'I do enjoy going to these clubs, though. Also, you get many more men than women in them, which I think is great because you get the men clustering around you, you get to be quite popular. I think that people who have got an unusual sexual interest know how vulnerable they are, and they're much less likely to be violent or difficult. The transvestite wasn't violent, he was over-insistent – I didn't have to hit him or anything like that. There are many heterosexual men who I've known who've been more insistent than that. People with unusual tastes tend to be a bit more careful.

'It's very sad that you get police raiding fetish clubs and swinging clubs, which they've been doing for years. Though running such a club is not illegal, the police make life very difficult for people who agree to run a night for whoever it might be. But swinging on the premises *is* illegal because that counts as running a disorderly house, which is a prostitution offence. The police behave as if they haven't got enough to do. They've got millions of real crimes to sort out, but do they? We were burgled when we were away on holiday and our neighbours very kindly interrupted the burglars and rang the police. But could they get them to come along? I bet you if there was a fetish club night going on at our house they'd have been round like a bloody shot. It makes me sick!'

With her tremendous enthusiasm for the subject of sex and her editorial talent, despite being female Isabel has risen rapidly in the world of legalised pornography. 'I'm now managing editor – I'm actually group managing editor for the company so I don't edit magazines but I manage them, so my level of involvement varies with the magazines. With *Penthouse* I see all the pages before they go to press. With *Forum* I have regular features meetings with the editor and staff to make sure that it's going in the right direction, and we get together and talk about ideas. For the other magazines I have more administrative and personnel-type responsibilities.'

Surprisingly for someone so uninhibited, she is often coy in her private life about her work. 'I don't always tell people what I do when I meet them socially. People always say things like, "How do you as a woman work for magazines that exploit women?" And I always say, "Well, I'm a woman, and I'm not exploited. I've never been on a *Penthouse* shoot where I've exploited a model or forced her into doing anything she didn't want to do." This is if people are interested – generally speaking, I try and avoid the subject, not because I don't want to talk about it but because it can be a bit boring, really. And a lot of people don't want to hear about it, anyway – they're not into pornography, which is fine. I just say that most women want to be looked at and admired and get dressed up to go out in the evenings, and really what a model gets from modelling, as well as getting paid better than she can be in many other jobs, is that feeling of having all the attention focused on her and knowing that she is going to be seen by hundreds of thousands, if not millions, of people. And that is tremendous. It makes her feel very feminine and very powerful, and I think most people understand that.'

Anyway, she maintains, anybody who says modelling isn't hard work doesn't know it from the inside. 'We were doing a shoot once for *Penthouse* in an old stately home in Surrey, which was beautiful. It was absolutely bloody freezing, and I was fully dressed! The models had a bit of a ghastly time. It wasn't a disaster because we had plenty of time to make it look good, but it was tricky trying to get enough hot water to put in the bath before it froze over – that was one of the scenes.

'But I don't think anyone is being exploited. The models love the attention, seeing their pictures in the magazines, or they wouldn't do it. If we ever thought anybody was even remotely uncertain about it we wouldn't touch them with a barge pole. And they've got to sign a model release [legal document consenting to the photographs of themselves being published] at the end of the session, anyway. If they don't sign that then we can't use the pictures.'

Isabel claims that there is no evidence to support the theory that pornography causes sexual crime such as rape. 'What evidence there is shows that, if anything, sex offenders, rapists and child-abusers are people who tend to have been abused themselves as children, and they tend to be people who have seen less pornography at a later age. That is in words of stone, so to speak, in the Howatt and Cumberbatch report that came out last December [1990]. It was a government-sponsored report. The Conservative government used two mainstream, non-controversial media psychologists to compile the report. They reviewed all the existing research that looked into links between pornography and violence and they came to the conclusion that there is no link, though they do think that more research needs to be done.

'People know that *Penthouse* is fantasy. They also know that they're not going to find pictures of women being raped or beaten or murdered, or any of the other ridiculous things that are talked about as being pornography. Why should a picture of an attractive woman make someone into a rapist? We're surrounded by images all the time. We grow up with all sorts of ideas about women and men, and as we grow up that's the most important influence on how we treat people later in life.

'We see far more violence in things that are on the news every day – why don't people get worried about that? Why don't they talk about things like the policeman getting murdered at the IRA funeral, when we witness the whole bloody catastrophe on the nine o'clock news? And yet people don't get excited about that – but they do as soon as you say "sex", or "pornography", which has become a very fashionable word. But what does "pornography" mean? It means sexually arousing material. And what's wrong with that? I think the anti-pornography people are frightened of their own sexuality in some way. If they are that frightened of other people getting turned on, what are they really saying? That they're frightened of getting turned on themselves? I also think that there isn't enough material for women.'

This reasoning, and the view that the absence of pornography for women is directly related to women's position in society, has led to the launching of a new magazine, which Isabel will also manage, *For Women*. It is she, not the actual editor, who is a man, who has been doing the extensive publicity for the new venture, appearing daily on chat shows and cropping up in nearly every newspaper. That, she says, is true liberation. The magazine will include features and profiles not dissimilar to those in many existing women's magazines, but will also carry many and varied photographs of nubile men with no clothes on – though, disappointingly, the showing of clear arousal in men is not allowed in this country. 'We'll have to work up to that', she promised an embarrassed male DJ with a nervous laugh, on Greater London Radio.

Between sips of black coffee, and after a polite refusal to eat any more of the croissants I'd ordered on the grounds that she was dieting in order to be able to fit into her costume for the forthcoming Sex Maniac's Ball, she explained about the material currently on offer. '*Forum* appeals to both sexes, but visually it doesn't have a huge amount to offer. *Playgirl* is very much a gay magazine – you know, orang-utan men or pretty little girls. Well, most women want something more main-stream masculine or feminine. There are rules that are unfair – you can't show an erection. Well, why not? You can show a woman looking sexually aroused. So there are unfairnesses, but I think people should recognise that and say there should be more erotic material around instead of trying to get rid of what they've already got. The situation is very different in Europe. If you go to a number of countries with a tradition of no sex before marriage etc., you can buy hard-core porno-graphy quite openly, even in newsagents. Nobody turns a hair.'

The other thing she was quick to point out about the anti-porn people is that they don't actually like anybody else to have a good time sexually. 'I don't know whether it's because they're not having a very good time themselves, or they are and they don't like anybody else doing anything different that might be more fun. There's an awful lot of jealousy and resentment of people enjoying themselves. And that's why people love reading about gay people getting Aids, because they think: Well, that serves them right, they've had thousands of lovers, a lot more fun, haven't had to worry about having children.'

Isabel is appalled by this attitude, which is often construed as a particularly British one: 'I think we're still a very insular nation. That's how the tabloids can run things like "Tide of filth coming into the country in 1992", which isn't true anyway. But there's this awful fear that we're going to be contaminated by what comes from outside. Why should sexual material be contaminating? Why should something that comes from abroad be contaminating? I do think that British people tend to be hung up about it – the Christian ethic obviously has got a lot to do with it. But then why that doesn't work in Catholic countries I don't know, apart from Ireland. Maybe in Latin countries people enjoy life more, drinking wine, having sex . . .

'In this country people often talk about the sanctity of the family and say we've got to protect our children from video nasties and porn, and yet in countries like Italy and Spain where the family is very close they don't have that. Somehow a close family life is perfectly able to co-exist with hard-core pornography being available in ordinary newsagents.'

Isabel met her husband, an economist working for BP, when already in her thirties, at a concert. She didn't immediately want to tell him what she did for a living, not because she was ashamed of it but because she finds that it's often better if people get to know her first for herself, and only subsequently learn what she does. 'But he immediately said, "Oh, you must work for a sex magazine!" ' She can't think how he could have guessed. 'I suppose he was just intuitive. Well, on the first few dates all we did was talk about sex. I think it was good, because he was able to ask all sorts of questions about my job, and ask me a few personal questions as well. I asked him questions as well, and we had a good time. It was actually a very nice way in. It does rather cut out the pussy-footing around.'

Having a family is something that she hopes will be a part of her life in the future, and she intends to maintain a liberated, enlightened home. 'I'd be absolutely honest about my work, and I'd try to answer their questions as they ask them. I'm not ashamed of anything I've done. It's made me a stronger person, in not feeling as inhibited about sex as perhaps I used to be, even though I didn't think I was. And that's very important. I think most people are still screwed up about sex to some extent and anything that can help prevent that happening has got to be a good thing.'

As a single girl she had lots of boyfriends. 'I haven't had thousands of lovers,' she confesses, 'but I did go out with a lot of people. I found men very interesting – almost everybody was interesting to go out with for one evening. I had a lot of sex when I was younger, and sometimes had two or three or even four lovers at once. When I say at once, I mean not in the same room, just over the same time. I really enjoyed that because in my teens and twenties I was always looking for the next man round the corner. I didn't want to settle down and be faithful to anyone, because I'd always be thinking about somebody else, I'd always want sexual variety in my life.

'It was only really when I got into my early thirties that I began to think perhaps, over the next few years, I should consider settling down. I found that I'd had enough casual sex, and I'd had enough uncommitted sex. Some of the relationships I'd had were very long, went on for three or four years and were full of love as well. It wasn't all casual – it was a good range of relationships – but I just felt in the end that I'd done that and wanted something lasting. I got married when I was nearly thirty-four, now I'm thirty-six. Having thought that I always wanted something different, a different man, and different sex – the ultimate fuck – I just felt that I'd had enough of that, and what would be different for me, and exciting, would be a really committed relationship.

'Jonathon is the fifteenth person who asked me to marry him. I'm sure that some of those people were not entirely serious, but over the years I have had my fair share. I think that was maybe because I wasn't dependent. I was a bit more fun, or a bit more energetic, than the average woman, and it helps if you actually like sex as well. I think that men find that very attractive. If men come across a woman who is sexually interested, and responsive, and perhaps willing to do a bit and initiate it herself, they feel like a real man.

'Having got married so late in life, I really do think I knew what I was doing. I knew what I was giving up, if you like, though I didn't feel that I was giving anything up because I felt that I'd had enough of that anyway, before I met Jonathon. I think with most people there is too much pressure to get married young. Possibly there's a case for having children when you're younger – it certainly is better physically. But to be completely and utterly tied up with three children by the time you're twenty-one often makes for such a miserable existence. People look at the divorce rates and say, "We should make divorce less easy", or "People don't take marriage seriously enough." People do take marriage seriously but they're often too young. People have got to enjoy themselves. You often get marriages breaking up because they haven't had enough sexual variety. If they had sexual variety in their youth they would get it out of their system in the way that I've done – at least some people, not all. Some people will always be congenitally promiscuous.'

But there is still a double standard relating to women's sexuality. It is still much easier for a man to be open than a woman, easier to be a man about town than a girl about town – though Isabel does see an improvement in men's attitudes towards women. 'Also, with the current fashions and the threat of Aids, having slept with thousands of others is actually not very appealing. People want to feel that the person they are with has been discriminating, because somehow that makes them feel that there is less chance of them getting HIV. I know that this is ridiculous – illogical, if you like – but I don't think we'll ever return to that Sixties thing of "I've had hundreds of lovers." Or maybe, when we've found a cure for Aids.'

For Isabel, pornography remains a business, and the magazines that she is responsible for are all legal and above board. There is no element of crime, no exploitation. 'I suppose you must get some unscrupulous people in the business, as you get in any business in the world. But to assume, as people do who are against pornography, that people are forced into it – it just isn't true. Some people say that it's the men being exploited, by buying pictures of women. Why do they need to see pictures of naked women so much? The power is in the woman's court.'

10

Exploiting your sexuality without being embarrassed about it

At a recent Friday night dinner, essentially a celebration of the Jewish Sabbath at the parental home of a close friend, and for the most part dedicated to sombre prayers and reflections on the past week, more than a dozen people were seated around a long formal dining table. Seated at the end of the table farthest away from our potentially disapproving hostess, a much younger sister of my friend, to my surprise, began a rather incongruous discussion in hushed tones about *For Women*. She had read some of the publicity about this new pornographic magazine for women and intrigued by the subject of my work was interested to hear my views. I felt women didn't really want or need that kind of male-orientated *Playboy* format to make them equal, I said. The conversation that ensued contained something of Nina Lopez-Jones's view of the equalising of the prostitution laws: the English Collective of Prostitutes campaigns for the abolition of the prostitution laws altogether, not for the extension of the laws to include the clients, as is now the case. She and her colleagues seek to be equalised 'up', she had explained when we met, so that prostitution would not be the business of the law at all, rather than 'down', to the position where both prostitute and client would be committing a crime. Women would probably prefer there to be no pornographic magazines at all, I suggested, rather than to be bombarded with explicit and rampant centrefolds of men.

An attractive divorcee in her forties with flame-coloured hair disagreed. 'You're still too young to know what it's like not to have plenty of potential lovers available to you,' she chided. 'There are many women who want to look at these magazines.

And look at the popularity of the Chippendales [the raunchy dance ensemble of well oiled male strippers].'

'But who on earth goes to see the Chippendales?' I countered.

'I did,' she replied.

Women are becoming more aggressive and open in the expression of their sexual needs. This is true not only of the women who are entrepreneurs in the business of selling sex – the current climate is one in which most women feel they are able, without fear of ridicule, to be outspoken on the subject. And they are clearly less reticent than ever about using their bodies and their sexuality for their own pleasure or gain. But the process of emancipation is not complete. Perhaps it will take the relegation of men to sex objects, and the advent of more female-orientated pornographic magazines full of naked and aroused men, to tip the balance between the sexes and bring about equality and a wider-reaching change in attitudes.

Today, thinking young women are getting together to talk about their sexuality. In London I came across a group of middle-class career women in their twenties who call themselves the Pussy Posse. They argue that being liberated entails a responsibility to have fun, to be proud of your body and to practise safe sex. They communicate this through the raucous, all-female gatherings that they hold. At one such event, at the Turkish baths at the Porchester Centre in Bayswater, organiser Farika, clad only in sunflowers – glued on to her breasts and bottom – led a demonstration of how to put a condom on a man without him knowing. She used a condom tucked into her mouth, and a cucumber. This game led to some success and much hilarity, though when I tried putting a Durex in my mouth it tasted so foul that I immediately spat it out again. They, however, maintain a relentless enthusiasm: 'Never be afraid to say, "That thing's not coming in without a jacket on!" '

In all the issues I have looked at in this book – the professional life of the stripper; the escort business; the selling of massage and sexual intercourse and all things imaginable in between; the high-profile involvement of women in the publication of pornographic magazines and videos; female sexual liberation – financial independence remains a crucial factor. It is financial independence that itself allows for sexual adventuring. So on the one hand, looking at sex as a business, it all comes down to being able to make a living by exploiting your sexuality without being embarrassed about it. But on the other, it is about a dramatic change in rights and attitudes.

This doesn't always work out as the women involved might have hoped. Many sexually related activities are still illegal. As I write this chapter, Linzi Drew has received a four-month prison sentence for running a mail order business selling hardcore pornographic videos, together with her boyfriend who has been sentenced to nine months. Apparently, Linzi's role in the crime was to write a sexy summary of the films, which had titles like *Jet Sex, Vanessa's Excess* and *Maximum Perversion*, to encourage orders. Police descriptions of the videos mentioned a man with a padlock on his penis and a sausage being used for sexual stimulation. The *Sunday Sport*, that paragon of British morality, gloated at length: '. . . one scene shows five men queuing up to take it in turns for a pretty, dark-haired beauty to suck their willies. . .'

But not all women have ceased to be victims. Not long ago, while waiting for a train at King's Cross, I went into the Casey Jones hamburger bar, and with some subconscious gesture towards the research for this book, sat down at the same table as a pale young woman who was wearily eating some chips. At first I failed to notice that at the next table sat three young women and a small child, all engaged in noisy conversation. Then a fourth joined them, and sat opposite me. In loud and Scottish tones she told them how her pimp had beaten her up; and she bent her head towards them to show the marks. Transfixed by the vividness of the girl's description and by her aggressive yet compelling manner, I listened – I hoped, discreetly. I was startled when she continued, looking meaningfully at me, 'It's the fault of all these yuppies. They're the ones that keep us here.' She challenged me: 'I bet you look down on me.' I said I did not look down on her, but in fact admired her for having the guts to do the work that she did. This seemed to relax the atmosphere a little, and the others joined in the conversation. Two worked another patch, and had merely come to King's Cross on a social visit. The Scottish girl told me she had been abused by her father and brother from the age of two until she was twelve: 'Because I looked like my mum, and she'd walked out. I went on the game when I was twelve, to escape.' She was now thirty.

The first, pale, woman joined in at this point, claiming that she too had been abused. But she wasn't a prostitute, she said. From the way she called us all 'sister', it sounded as if she'd found feminism in the way that some people find religion. I asked the Scottish girl if she'd rather be doing something else. She said she would. 'But what else can I do? I've never done anything else and I've got no qualifications.' She was on drugs. Her mistrust of men was intense. 'I had a boyfriend for a year and a half. He was a lawyer, picked me up and then fell in love with me. Told me all this crap, and then he dumped me. What did he go and do that for?' None of them seemed to agree whether prostitution should be legalised or not, and when I mentioned the English Collective of Prostitutes they had never heard of it.

This casual encounter brought home to me the desperate life still led by women on the streets. There are many young, disadvantaged women who become the victims of a less than caring society. But there are also those women, like Bella and Paula, who take control of their lives and are able to get on in society, using their minds – and their bodies.

In these last years of the twentieth century, in our Western societies, the climate exists for more and more women to lead lives of their own choosing. The feminist movement has broken down many barriers in all areas of society, and in the sex industry the scope has never been greater. While a sad and depressing underclass still exists, particularly in the recession of the 1990s, the outlook for women involved in selling sex is, ironically, quite positive.